THE GREAT GOLDWYN

*This is a volume in the
Arno Press collection*

ASPECTS OF FILM

Advisory Editor
Garth S. Jowett

*See last pages of this volume
for a complete list of titles.*

THE
GREAT GOLDWYN

ALVA JOHNSTON

ARNO PRESS
A New York Times Company
New York • 1978

Editorial Supervision: MARIA CASALE

———◆———

Reprint Edition 1978 by Arno Press Inc.

ASPECTS OF FILM
ISBN for complete set: 0-405-11125-8
See last pages of this volume for titles.

Manufactured in the United States of America

———◆———

Library of Congress Cataloging in Publication Data

Johnston, Alva.
　The great Goldwyn.

　(Aspects of film)
　Reprint of the ed. published by Random House,
New York.
　1. Goldwyn, Samuel, 1882-1974. 2. Moving-
picture producers and directors--United States--
Biography. I. Title. II. Series.
[PN1998.A3G66 1978]　791.43'0232'0924　[B]
ISBN 0-405-11133-9　　　　　　　77-11377

RANDOM HOUSE

presents

RANDOM HOUSE - NEW YORK

COPYRIGHT, 1937,
BY RANDOM HOUSE, INC., NEW YORK
PRINTED IN UNITED STATES OF AMERICA

THE
GREAT GOLDWYN

By ALVA JOHNSTON

Starring

SAMUEL GOLDWYN

*and a huge supporting cast
of Hollywood Stars*

Written and Directed by:
ALVA JOHNSTON

Produced by:
BENNETT A. CERF
ROBERT K. HAAS
DONALD S. KLOPFER

Assistant Director
in Charge of Editorial Matters:
SAXE COMMINS

Assistant Director
in Charge of Production:
HERBERT R. CAHN

Settings:
(Typography, Binding & Jacket)
ANDOR BRAUN & VALENTI ANGELO

COPYRIGHT, 1937,
BY RANDOM HOUSE, INC., NEW YORK

TECHNICAL PRODUCTION:
American Book Bindery–Stratford Press, Inc.

THE
GREAT GOLDWYN

1

THE ELECTION OF WOODROW WILSON CHANGED Samuel Goldwyn from a glove salesman to a movie magnate. The Wilson Administration lowered the tariff on skins. Sam thought that would take the profit out of gloves. He looked around for some other line and picked the movies.

That was in 1913. Sam was only thirty, but he had been a glove salesman for fifteen years. He had sold gloves to Yankee general-store proprietors. He had a sales enthusiasm bordering on frenzy. Sam argues a man into a coma or into a disorder resembling "bends." His victim signs anything.

Sam talked a large part of Hollywood into existence.

The great Paramount studio is a monument to his nuisance value. The Metro-Goldwyn-Mayer plant is largely the petrified conversation of Goldwyn. His voice breaks men down like a rubber hose. He has tortured vast quantities of talent and capital into Hollywood.

Sam is out of the two giant organizations which he played a large part in forming. He is out because the ruling principle of his life is—Goldwyn is boss. Sam is the absolute monarch. Paramount made the mistake of not accepting this principle, and it lost Goldwyn. Metro-Goldwyn-Mayer made the identical error, and it lost Sam too.

Sam then organized his third company, in which he is as absolute as Ivan the Terrible. This is Samuel Goldwyn, Inc., Ltd. He owns 100 per cent of it. He quit the Hays organization because he would not let Will Hays or anyone else encroach on his sovereignty. He withdrew from the Central Casting Agency because he wanted to pick his own actors, even for the smallest parts. He was the first producer to establish his own wardrobe; he wanted to control the last detail of his costuming. From the beginning of his career, Sam was regarded as the greatest salesman in the business. Later he was called the smartest publicity man and general showman. In the last ten or twelve years he has won increasing fame as an artist. He

THE GREAT GOLDWYN

has a long history of producing pictures of high quality, like *Stella Dallas, The Dark Angel, Arrowsmith, These Three,* and *Dodsworth.* Sam has had more fights than any other man in Hollywood. Because he is a rebel and a trail blazer in the use of the English language, he is the central figure of a great comic legend.

But most of those who hate him or laugh at him will say, "I admire Sam." The routine is to ridicule Goldwyn for a while and to denounce him for a while, and then to credit him with "an instinctive love of beauty" and "complete" or "almost complete artistic integrity." The ablest people in Hollywood, generally speaking, admire Goldwyn most. His closest friend was the late Irving Thalberg. It is almost a fad in Hollywood today to rave about Goldwyn's taste. He commands respect because of a seeming contempt for money when he is in a mood to lavish it in the pursuit of what he regards as perfection. He suffers and agonizes to get "the Goldwyn touch"; those who work for him suffer and agonize with him.

His greatest fame, however, is based on Goldwyn sayings and Goldwyn jokes. Sam's words built much of Hollywood, but he mispronounces them and uses them in the wrong places. Nouns, verbs and adjectives are Goldwyn's tools; he is more celebrated for broken tools than for what he accomplished with them. He is unrivaled today, as an unconscious humorist, or wit, through no fault of his own. Sam does not wholly enjoy his pre-eminence, although at times he has deliberately promoted it. Henry Ford collected Ford jokes and printed them as advertising matter; on that precedent Goldwyn's publicity department formerly collected and invented Goldwyn gags and circulated them. The trend had already been so well established, however, that any dazzling flash of ignorance or any startling disarrangement of words would ultimately be attributed to Sam without any help from his press representatives. Today it takes an expert to pick the genuine Goldwyn lines from the spurious. More people are counterfeiting on Goldwyn than on Uncle Sam.

Some of the true Goldwyn lines are a credit to him. He can often put things more forcefully in his own medium of expression than they could possibly be said in the king's English. An ordinary man, on deciding to quit the Hays organization, might have turned to his fellow producers and said, "Gentlemen, I prefer to stand aloof," or "Gentlemen, I have decided to go my own way." Sam said, "Gentlemen, include me out." It would be impossible to make a more pointed remark than Goldwyn's, "A verbal contract isn't worth the paper it's written on." One day, after slicing five or six golf balls, he made a

THE GREAT GOLDWYN

beautiful drive; he turned to the caddy and asked, "What did I do right?" The true Goldwyn line is seldom a boner or a howler. It is usually a plain statement with a slight twist; as, for example, his exclamation at the beach one lovely Sunday morning, "What a wonderful day to spend Sunday!"

Sam commands legitimate attention by thinking strange thoughts rather than uttering strange words. The absolute-monarch psychology causes him to feel that his problems are world problems. When he meditates, he thinks that everyone should, by some telepathic process, be listening in. He awakened an assistant at midnight once and started a telephone conversation by saying, "The woman must die in the end." "What woman?" the man asked. Goldwyn had been thinking out the plot of a picture; the employee was expected to know by thought transference all that had gone before. Sam was as annoyed as if the man had gone to sleep in a conference. He expects employees to have a sixth sense and to render supernatural service. Again and again, Sam starts conversations without telling the other man what the subject is.

One day he stopped every man he met on the Goldwyn lot, asking: "Do you think it is raining tonight?"

Several said, "No."

One man said, "Of course not. There's not a cloud in the sky."

Sam withered him with a look. "I mean in New York," he said. "Our picture opens tonight in New York."

One of the leading directors in Hollywood called on Goldwyn one day at Goldwyn's request. As the man entered the office, Sam pounded his fist on his desk and said: "I won't pay you a cent more."

"Why, you haven't paid me anything yet," said the director.

"I don't mean that," said Sam. "I mean I know what you have been getting and I won't pay you a cent more."

The director still looked blank. With a sigh, Goldwyn went back and laid the foundation for the conversation by explaining that he wanted the director to make a picture for him; the interview then started all over again. Much of the time Sam's mind is so concentrated on pictures that he is practically in a trance. One day he stopped over in Chicago, went to the Hotel Blackstone, registered, went directly to his room, seized the telephone and said, "Get my office." He expected the operator, without even knowing his name, to connect him with his studio in Hollywood. The operator took Goldwyn by surprise by asking the number. He didn't know it.

Sam has a prodigious memory, but he doesn't know

his telephone number. He doesn't know his home address. He will not charge his mind with points of this kind. Once when he was driving with Harpo Marx, Sam wanted to stop and telephone home. "What's my number?" he asked. Harpo gave it to him. A moment later, Sam asked again. Harpo repeated it. "Write it down for me, Harpo," said Sam. He wouldn't ask his memory to retain a detail of that kind from the car to a telephone. He never forgets a point relating to his primary interest, the pictures. Conversations of years ago on this subject are stored away in his mind like phonograph records, but he won't burden his memory with things that others can remember for him. Sam is the king, and the other people are his faithful vassals. No one is too big for the office of king's remembrancer. Sam Harris, the famous Broadway producer, got the appointment years ago. Harris, Arthur Hopkins, Goldwyn and others had been playing golf. In the dressing room, Harris put on a distinguished suit of underwear.

"Where did you get it?" asked Goldwyn. Harris told him. "I'm going to get some," said Goldwyn. "Call me up tomorrow morning and remind me of it."

Anyone who happens to be with Sam automatically becomes the chancellor of the king's exchequer. Sam never carries money. He is slender and an elegant dresser. Bills make a bulge in the coat pocket. Small change makes a bulge in the vest pocket. Sam is too proud of his figure and his tailor to allow his lines to be distorted by currency in any form.

Most of Sam's word trouble is inattention. His mind is usually 90 or 100 per cent occupied with future pictures. He won't use his brain for non-essentials like other men's names, and he has an undiscriminating ear for sounds. Only one syllable out of three in an ordinary man's name will register correctly in Sam's consciousness; a world celebrity might score two out of three. In the very act of telling Louis Bromfield how important the name of Bromfield was, Sam called him Bloomfield. When hiring Arthur Hornblow, Jr., Sam called him Hornbloom. Hornblow wrote the name on a paper; Sam waved it aside, saying, "Show me later." Ben Cahane, a member of the Goldwyn organization, was always "Mr. Cocoon." When Charlie Chaplin returned from Paris several years ago, Sam inquired after the health of Anatole France by asking, "How are the Affairs of Anatole?" Shirley Temple is Anne Shirley to Goldwyn; King Vidor is Henry King.

Sam pays fabulous salaries to Big Names, but he reserves the right to mispronounce them. He worships writers. Many of the best of them have worked for him.

THE GREAT GOLDWYN

It has been said that if Shakespeare were alive today, Goldwyn would have him. It is an interesting notion; some of the bad plays, like *Cymbeline*, *Troilus and Cressida*, and *Pericles*, might have been tightened up into great dramas if the playwright had had a producer over him to tell him, "It stinks, Wagspeare. It's lousy. It's terrible. It's ghastly. You're ruining me, Wagstaff."

Sam's passionate concentration on his primary purposes leaves only a few fibers of his brain for secondary matters. That causes his scrambled phonetics; it also gives him a genius for making unexpected comments. A story conference on *Barbary Coast* was being held at Goldwyn's home one fine morning. A fierce wrangle had developed, with floor pacing and table pounding. William Wellman, the director, happened to pass a window. He stopped and looked out.

"That's the most beautiful sight I ever saw," he said. The others quit fighting and came over to the window. A mother quail and a flock of baby quail were trotting across the lawn.

"Think of us wrangling here when we could be looking at things like that," said one of the conferees.

"It's the prettiest thing I ever saw," said another. It was now Sam's turn to say something.

"They don't belong here," said Sam. He didn't say it

in bad humor. He didn't resent the quail's trespassing. It was merely his turn to speak and he contributed a point of information.

The first impression of Goldwyn that you get in Hollywood is that he spends all his time hewing away at the dictionaries and grammars. The second is that he is always in a frenzy; he is said to be the only man who can run amuck sitting down. Both impressions are exaggerated. Many persons who know Sam pretty well have never heard him miscoin a phrase; others have never found him anything but reasonable. He never forgets that Sam is king, but he is able to remember that something is due to princes of the blood, which is his rating of people of talent. He is not in a hurry; no producer gives more time to writers and directors; he can be not only patient but long-suffering. He has accepted kidding by Eddie Cantor and other illustrious wags with the tolerance of a monarch toward his licensed jesters. He will do anything for the cause, which is to turn out good pictures. His great rages and furies are generally intended as contributions to the cause.

He is second to none in his respect for money, but he will throw it away like a madman to get the effect he wants in a picture. When he didn't like his first version of *Nana*, he scrapped it completely, throwing away with-

THE GREAT GOLDWYN

out a murmur the $411,000 he had spent on it; his own money, too, not stockholders'. He will not let down the name of Goldwyn, if he can help it. His failures are not the result of any lack of striving.

Goldwyn's usual method is to pay an enormous price for the screen rights—$165,000 for *Dead End;* $160,000 for *Dodsworth*—of a stage hit or popular novel, and then to hire the best writers and directors to make it. His ability as a producer is sometimes discounted, on the theory that he buys success. This is not the whole story, however. He has turned out distinguished pictures over a long period. Hundreds have collaborated with him, but Sam has been able to place his unmistakable mark on all his work. The greatest tribute to him is that the phrase "the Goldwyn touch" is part of the vocabulary of Hollywood. "The Goldwyn touch" is not brilliance or sensationalism. It is something that manifests itself gradually in a picture; the characters are consistent; the workmanship is honest; there are no tricks and short cuts; the intelligence of the audience is never insulted. Goldwyn ran away from his home in Poland at the age of eleven and arrived here alone in the steerage at the age of thirteen. His education in English was a year at night school. With this background, the most impressive fact about him is his development of taste and artistic conscience;

today it is a compliment to nearly any picture to say that it looks like a Goldwyn production.

Goldwyn is sometimes called a Napoleon—a title of no distinction in Hollywood. It is like calling a man "Mister." Sam has, however, a belief in his star, or a belief that the universe is rigged in his favor. He can't understand losing at games of chance or in business controversies; it is a violation of the laws of nature as he understands them, and it makes him the hardest kind of a loser. He stated his philosophy when he had an argument with another company over the services of William Anthony McGuire, who wrote The Great Ziegfeld. Sam wanted McGuire badly. So did the other producer. Both sides claimed to have him under contract. The only solution was arbitration.

"All right," said Sam. "I'm a fair man. I'll submit anything to arbitration. But remember, no matter what is decided, McGuire goes to work for me."

When Goldwyn loses at games, there are stormy scenes. It is not the loss of money that hurts; it's the sacrilege. Such things can't happen legitimately in the Goldwyn universe; foul play is indicated. There sometimes is foul play. Goldwyn-baiting is a recognized pastime. Some of his dearest friends cheat him because they like to hear him rave. Backgammon, as Sam plays it with some members of his circle, is as honest as wrestling. Chico Marx said, "Sam is the only man in the world who can throw a seven with one die." Charles MacArthur once slapped Sam's hand and said, "That's cheating." "What's that between us?" said Sam.

Sam once kicked a lot of stones out of the way and made a path smooth as a billiard table in front of his golf ball, which was lying near the green. Then he tapped it, almost making the hole. His opponent, Harpo Marx, kicked a stone out of the way of his own ball.

"You can't do that!" shouted Sam.

"But you just did it," said Harpo.

"But didn't you hear my caddy say I shouldn't?" demanded Sam.

Sam loses pretty regularly at bridge, so fights are frequent. There was an uproar at the bridge table on Joseph Schenck's yacht one day. Schenck walked to the other end of the yacht, where the wives of the players were sitting, and said, "They're having a fight."

"Sam and who?" inquired Mrs. Goldwyn.

Sam scolded his partner, Constance Bennett, once for overbidding her hand.

"How did I know you had nothing?" she asked.

"Didn't you hear me keeping still?" asked Sam.

At another bridge party on the Schenck yacht, Sam

went down eight hundred points on one play. He insisted that it should be only seven hundred. In the argument that followed, Sam offered to bet Edwin Loeb, a Hollywood lawyer, one hundred dollars that it should be seven hundred points.

"I won't bet," said Loeb. "It would be betting on a sure thing."

Sam scoffed and jeered, and finally forced the bet. The book was consulted; Sam was wrong. He paid the one hundred dollars under protest.

"You were betting on a sure thing," he said.

Later in the same game the same point came up. Sam insisted the play set him back only seven hundred. He badgered Loeb into another one-hundred-dollar bet; lost; paid under protest; claimed he was the victim of a sure thing.

Next to his royal and imperial cast of mind, Sam's chief trait is his love of battle. Both traits were necessary to enable him, with his unpromising start in life, to carve his career. He is one of the pioneers of the modern motion picture, and he is still giving lessons in the art to the new generation. If he were a less impressive figure, the Goldwyn gag would be unknown. A smaller man can utter misbegotten bons mots by the hundreds without being noticed. It is useless today for anybody else to be witty unawares. Sam has cornered the world supply of unconscious humor. Everything from Irish bulls to Japanese-schoolboy comedy is credited to him.

Before Sam arrived in Hollywood, the official unconscious humorists were two brothers who made short comic pictures. The brothers became obscure; Sam became famous. The old anecdotes deserted the brothers and attached themselves to Goldwyn. "Our comedies are not to be laughed at" is one of the lines that abandoned the original author and joined the Goldwyn legend. Another was a telegram sent by one of the brothers after their studio had burned: "If there is nothing left to watch, fire the watchman." When a director asked the brothers to send him to the Rockies to shoot cliffs and forests, the reply was, "A rock's a rock and a tree's a tree; shoot it in Griffith Park." The brothers were robbed of these and other gags; Goldwyn became the reluctant receiver of the stolen goods.

"I can answer you in two words, 'Im possible,' " is almost the cornerstone of the Goldwyn legend, but Sam did not say it. It was printed late in 1925 in a humorous magazine and credited to an anonymous Potash or Perlmutter. An executive in the Chaplin studio pointed it out to Charlie Chaplin, saying, "It sounds like Sam Goldwyn." Chaplin said, "We'll pin it on Sam," and he repeated it until it became a world-famous Goldwynism. "I read part of it all the way through," had a similar origin. A producer said that to a team of writers. They laughed. The producer said, "Boys, I've always been good to you. Don't tell it on me. I'm sensitive. Tell it on Sam." It would have pinned itself on Sam in the course of time, anyway. The sun-dial story, which is having a vogue now, runs:

"What's that?" asks Sam.

"A sun-dial."

"What's it for?" asks Sam.

"It tells time by the sun."

"My, my, what won't they do next?"

This was printed years ago as the saying of a gardener. It gravitated slowly to California and finally attached itself to Goldwyn. Probably the most actively circulated Goldwyn story today is that someone said, "What beautiful hands your wife has," and that Sam replied, "Yes, I'm going to have a bust made of them." So many persons swear they overheard this that Sam must have said it over the radio; but many authorities say it has not the genuine Goldwyn stamp. There are reliable witnesses who are sure they heard Sam say, "It rolls off my back like a duck," when Sam's publicity man showed him a bunch of newspaper reviews damning one of his pictures.

THE GREAT GOLDWYN

Charles MacArthur, a Goldwyn expert, challenged its authenticity.

A kind of Goldwyn scholarship has grown up; there are specialists who can detect fake Goldwynisms as an archaeologist can spot a phony Greek vase. The duck's-back line was alleged to lack the Goldwyn rhythm. Later it came to light that it had been invented at the Goldwyn studio restaurant. Members of the staff had amused themselves at lunch every day for a week by trying to say things as Sam might have said them. They produced scores of damaged maxims, malformed proverbs and mangled metaphors. The duck's-back line was considered the only one to have the master touch, but it was not good enough to fool experts.

One of the standard Goldwyn lines was plagiarized from George M. Cohan. "Never let that —— in this office again," shouted Cohan; then, feeling a little ridiculous and turning the joke against himself, he added, "unless we need him." The conscious humor is omitted from the line as transplanted to Goldwyn, who is supposed to have said, "Never let that —— on this lot again unless we need him." Sam did act on this principle in the case of Ben Hecht. He issued a statement to the effect that he would never employ him again and that no other studio would. Hecht had not only offended Goldwyn but had deprived him of revenge. After the trouble, Hecht had got to the newspapers first with a statement to the effect that the Hollywood producers were high-minded art lovers, while the writers were squalid racketeers, and so on. Hecht had expounded Goldwyn's case so convincingly that the producer had nothing left to add.

Sam's reply was a boycott. But he soon decided that he needed Hecht and his writing partner, MacArthur. He not only swallowed his indignation but he signed a contract which stipulated that he was not allowed to speak to them. For three weeks Goldwyn observed this clause. Then he violated it by telephoning to MacArthur on the pretext that Mrs. Goldwyn desired to know where to address a letter to MacArthur's wife, Helen Hayes. After some other disarming inquiries, Sam asked how the writers were getting on with their script. MacArthur broke down and said, "All right."

"That's great. That's wonderful," said Sam. He then sent his regards to the "racketeer," as he called Hecht, and the feud was over.

Goldwyn has had a long succession of able press agents from Harry Reichenbach to his present publicity chief, Jock Lawrence. Nearly all the Alumni of the Goldwyn press department are distinguished people. Under Sam they learned how to work publicity miracles. They boast of the terrific punishment they took under Goldwyn. They speak of Sam as they speak of operations. Goldwyn is like the English schoolmaster, Busby, who scourged his pupils into illustriousness. Sam gets more space in the papers than any man in Hollywood, but he regards himself as the victim of a conspiracy of silence. No one has heard good modern malediction unless he has heard Sam reproach a press agent for not performing enough miracles. For weeks after a conference with Sam, the publicity man is picking broken epigrams out of his skin.

Goldwyn's attitude toward publicity is logical. Pictures are everything to him. Pictures are man's only legitimate interest; pictures are Goldwyn Pictures. When people think of anything else, they're getting off the subject; the mission of his press department is to keep their attention from wandering. The Puritans had a functionary who went around tapping the heads of people they caught not listening to the sermon; Sam's publicity men are expected to crack down on anyone they catch not thinking of Goldwyn. When Sam finds a newspaper full of wars, floods and crimes, he is furious with his publicity department for letting digressions and irrelevances leak in. The Goldwyn press agent does not expect praise in proportion to the amount of Goldwyn stuff in the newspapers; he expects blame according to the percentage of non-Goldwyn stuff that gets in.

There have been different opinions as to the publicity value of Goldwyn gags. One school holds that any publicity is publicity, and any fame is fame. Acting on this principle, some of Sam's propagandists have raided vaudeville, radio and old joke books to plagiarize hot ones and hang them on their employer. The other school holds that "the Goldwyn touch" means intelligence, taste, class; and that it blurs the impression to represent Sam personally as the king of unconscious low comedy. After one of his trips to England, Goldwyn was inclined to take the latter view. Sam is an important social number in England and on the Continent. On one trip he found distinguished foreigners lionizing him to a degree that worried him. On his return, he ordered a change of policy in the publicity department. "Over there," he said, "they kept watching my mouth all the time, expecting something funny to pop out."

They were disappointed. Sam goes sometimes for days without saying anything memorable. He usually has to be pretty excited in order to coin anything that will live. He does have good days, however. Here are a few Goldwyn lines that are vouched for by good authorities:

"The trouble with this business is the dearth of bad pictures."

"We can get all the Indians we need at the reservoir."

"Our new executive was born in an orpheum asylum."

"My horse was in the lead, coming down the homestretch, when the caddy had to fall off."

"Excuse me, I am going out for some tea and trumpets."

"I have been laid up with intentional flu."

"He treats me like the dirt under my feet."

"That's the way with these directors, they're always biting the hand that lays the golden egg."

"You're always taking the bull between the teeth."

"For this part I want a lady, a lady; somebody that's couth."

"I would be sticking my head in a moose."

"I want to make a picture about the Russian Secret Police—the G. O. P."

"I had a monumental idea this morning, but I didn't like it."

He embarrassed a lady writer once by saying "cohabit" when he meant "co-operate."

"Will you give me your word of honor that you will work for me when you finish your present picture?"

Sam asked a writer. The writer said he couldn't. "If you can't give me your word of honor, will you give me your promise?" demanded Sam.

"It's too caustic," said a director, when asked his opinion of a script.

"To hell with the cost," replied Sam. "If it's a good picture, we'll make it."

2

THE FIRST LAW OF GOLDWYN'S BEING IS THAT Goldwyn is boss. He quickly gets out of anything that he can't boss. At the age of twelve, he got out of his family.

Sam was born in Warsaw in 1882 and went to work as an office boy when he was eleven. A year later he ran away to England. In order to be his own boss, he worked at the age of twelve as a blacksmith's helper. For a while he lived with relatives at Manchester. They tried to exercise authority over him, and at thirteen he crossed the Atlantic in the steerage. He preferred to operate in a hemisphere where he didn't have any relatives.

Sam went to work as a glovemaker in a factory at

Gloversville, New York. A year in night school was his only education in this country, but he succeeded in making himself a master of rhetoric. He uses words wrongly, but with magic power. The map of Hollywood has been transformed by Sam's gnarled eloquence.

Sam is a born aristocrat. By the time he was fifteen he was moving in the higher circles of the town. When he was seen on the street, he was either alone or in the company of some Gloversville celebrity. His most intimate friend was Abe Lehr, the heir-apparent of a glove king. Their friendship lasted, off and on, for forty years. When Sam became the Great Goldwyn of the films, Lehr was invaluable because he had opinions of his own and was not afraid to cross Sam. For example, when *Yes, Yes* had been tentatively selected as the title of one of Eddie Cantor's pictures, Lehr opposed it.

"What's the matter with that title?" demanded Goldwyn.

"I don't like it," said Lehr.

"Give me one reason why *Yes, Yes* is not a good title," said Sam.

"It's too negative," said Abe.

"And they claim I say funny things," said Sam. Abe had his way, however, and the title was changed.

The first business association between Sam and Abe

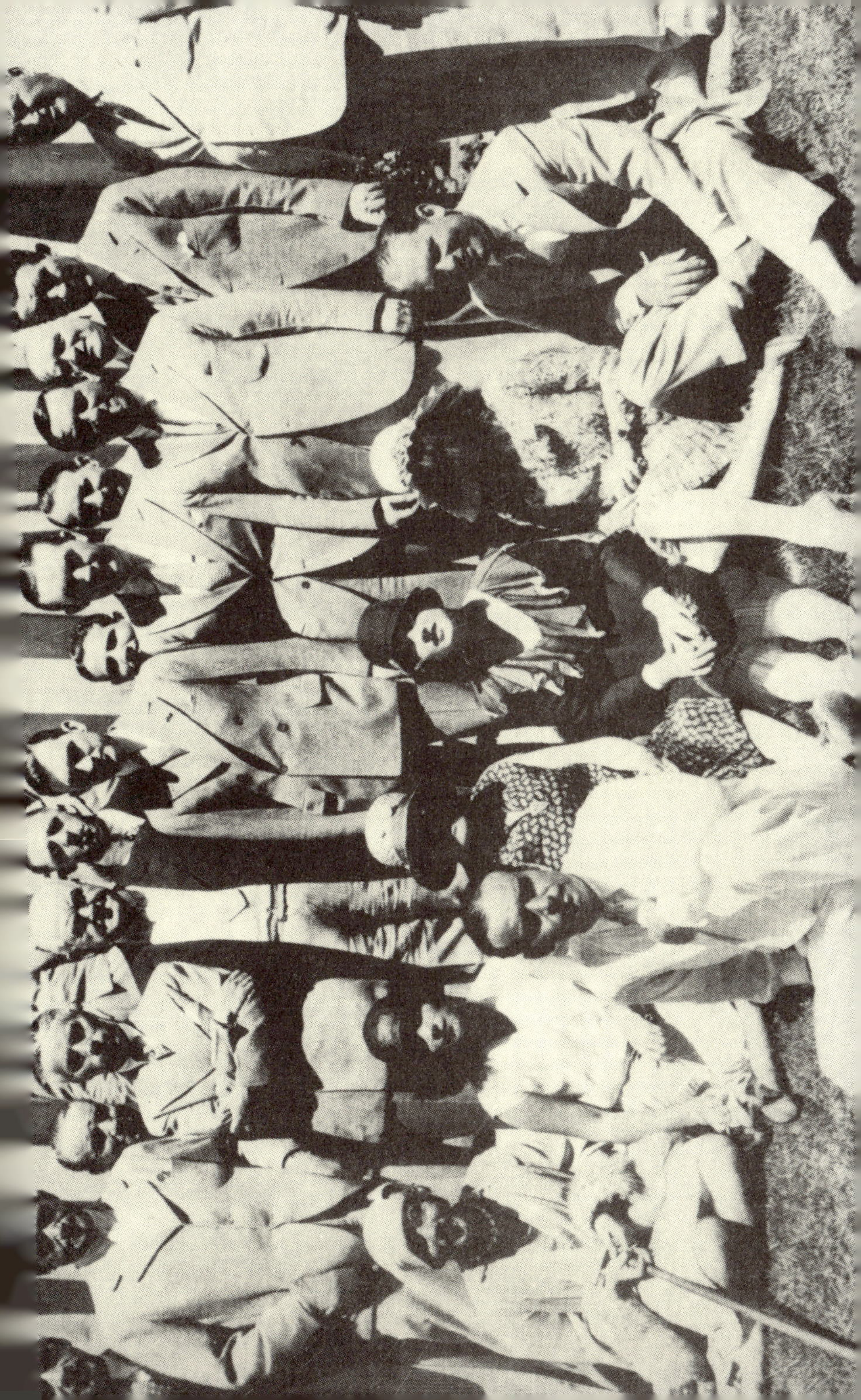

SAMUEL GOLDWYN
entertains for New York's Mayor Walker during Jimmy's visit to Hollywood several years ago. Douglas Fairbanks is seated in the foreground. The girl at the left is Lupe Velez, and next to her are Dolores Del Rio, Louella Parsons, and Marion Davies. Charlie Chaplin is next to Mr. Goldwyn. Two down from Jimmy Walker is Ernst Lubitsch.

occurred when they were working at the same bench in Abe's father's glove factory. Sam was industrious and Abe was lazy. They formed an arrangement under which Sam worked an hour more than the regular day and Abe worked an hour less than the regular day. In return for this, the proprietor's son, through his pull, caused the foreman to furnish Sam with the best skins. You can cut gloves out of good skins much faster than you can cut gloves out of bad skins. Sam was paid on a piecework basis. He made so much money that Lehr, Sr., investigated. He discovered the plot and fired both Abe and Sam. He relented later. "I'll take you back," he said, "but you can't work in partnership any more."

Abe Lehr learned, at Gloversville, a lesson that was invaluable to him in Hollywood—the lesson that it is a fatal error to do what Sam says and a fatal error not to do what he says. Sam took $120 from his pocket one night, kept twenty dollars for himself and then handed $100 to Abe, saying, "No matter what I say, don't give me this back till tomorrow." Sam quickly lost the twenty dollars at faro and then demanded another twenty dollars. Abe refused. Then Abe learned for the first time something of the true genius of his friend—his cyclonic emotional energy, his power to play on human weaknesses, his execrations, his wild heartbroken cries. The unnerved Abe surrendered twenty dollars after twenty dollars, until it was all gone. Then Sam, in a white heat, denounced Abe's breach of trust, lack of manhood, perfidy, treachery and insubordination. It was all good training for Abe in his later career as Sam's chief lieutenant in Hollywood.

At fifteen, Sam went on the road, selling gloves in small New England towns. The opportunity came to him by default. No other salesman wanted to tour the graveyard circuit and battle with the Yankee general-store proprietors. Sam had, at the age of ten, experienced a sudden feeling that he was a great man; others felt the same way about Sam when he made a success of his sales campaign among the Puritans. By the time he was eighteen, he was considered one of the great glove salesmen in the world. He then took two months off and went to Europe, meeting his mother at Karlsbad. Every year after that, Sam went abroad between sales trips. He developed his instinct for acquainting himself with important people. He educated himself by relentless inquisitiveness and by rare skill in searching other people's minds. In later life, Goldwyn never did become a Hollywood provincial; he is today as well informed on Europe as any man in the film capital. The young glove salesman had made his trips to Europe for pleasure, but they helped him later in understanding the foreign film market. Sam was so successful in selling pictures abroad that he was able, nearly fifteen years ago, to exclaim, "Gentlemen, I've invented a new slogan— Goldwyn pictures griddle the earth.'"

Sam's entrance into the films was an accident. In 1910 he married Blanche Lasky, who divorced him in 1915. She was a sister of Jesse Lasky, then a leading producer of vaudeville acts. In 1912, Lasky toyed with the idea of making films. He listened to Arthur S. Friend, a young New York lawyer, who had a prophetic sense of the future of pictures. Friend wanted Lasky to produce long films that unfolded romantic stories from the beginning to the end, even if they occupied the screen for an hour. Lasky was the man to do it, according to Friend, because Lasky knew vaudeville; a man who understood the mind of the vaudeville audience would understand the mind of the future film audience. The project was presented to Lasky at the wrong time, however. Lasky had just lost $100,000 in a new venture, the Folies-Bergère theater-restaurant in New York. It made him conservative. He wanted to stick to his own field—vaudeville. Friend then talked to Goldwyn, who was likewise cold. Sam had plans for starting a glove business of his own.

A year later Sam was ready to listen to Friend. The Democrats were in power; Sam thought that was bad for the glove business. He had also been impressed by a visit to a Herald Square movie house where *Broncho Billy*, a two-reel Western, was being shown. The place was packing them in; fresh stacks of dimes were harvested hourly. *Broncho Billy* inspired Goldwyn at first with the ambition to become a theater owner. He priced some theaters and found them out of reach. It seemed cheaper to make pictures than to exhibit them. Sam finally did adopt Friend's idea, and went mad about it. He nearly drove Lasky mad by his incessant repetition of the same arguments; incessancy being one of Sam's leading characteristics. He waylaid bankers and Broadway producers. When he talked of screen epics and twenty-five-cent admission charges, Goldwyn was thought to be suffering from hallucinations. The films were then in evil repute. The industry seemed to be a parasite on the white-slave traffic, the average screen masterpiece being a technical educational—exposé, it was called—in the use of knockout drops and poisoned needles. Also, the flickering of the films caused blinding headaches and a permanent squint, according to medical men. Goldwyn made his first dent in the wall of prejudice against the movies in October, 1913. On Columbus

Day he telephoned a friend to meet him at the Hoffman House.

"I've found a backer," said Sam. "He wants us to meet him with a prospectus. What's a prospectus?"

Friend drew up one on Hoffman House stationery, but the deal fell through. Sam continued to argue ceaselessly, day and night, with his brother-in-law. Lasky finally agreed to give his name, which was a big one in the amusement world, to the movie venture; but it was stipulated in writing that Lasky should not be bothered further on the subject. Friend, Lasky and Mr. and Mrs. Goldwyn contributed a total of $26,500, the entire capital on which the enterprise started. The company was called the Jesse L. Lasky Feature Picture Company. Friend took an active interest, but he had a law practice which kept him busy. Goldwyn was the only full-time worker. He had most of the labor and none of the glory; Sam had at that time a self-effacing streak which he conquered later.

Goldwyn's first move was characteristic; he tried to hire the greatest man in the business, D. W. Griffith. This was two years before *The Birth of a Nation*, but Griffith had already made the four-reel *Judith of Bethulia*, a landmark in the film history, and had already invented the close-up, fade-out, dissolve and practically all the camera technique in use today. "We want you with us," said Sam, explaining how his company planned to make one magnificent five-reeler every month, based on some famous play or novel.

Griffith regarded Sam as an irresponsible young megalomaniac. He said: "Show me $250,000 in the bank and we'll talk about it."

The job went to Cecil B. de Mille at $100 a week. De Mille was, at that time, an unhappy young playwright who was on the verge of going to Mexico to take part in the civil war. He started to make the first picture, *The Squaw Man*, at Flagstaff, Arizona, in order to be near the Indians, but moved on to Hollywood in order to be near people who knew how to grind a camera.

The original $26,500 did not pay the cost of production. Dustin Farnum, the hero of *The Squaw Man*, sensed failure and demanded $5000 cash, instead of a stock interest which would have been worth millions. Sam raised additional money by masterful salesmanship. He sold veteran film men all over the country the exhibition rights of *The Squaw Man* and eleven other unborn epics. He collected in advance.

"We're ruined," exclaimed Jesse Lasky at the first private showing of *The Squaw Man*. The actors appeared cut off at the waist, their legs walking in the air several feet above their heads. In a London drawing-room scene, the floor rose and the ceiling descended, crushing a mob of aristocrats like grapes in a wine press. Swarms of actors rose like quail and whizzed off the screen. Mountains twitched nervously and flitted away. The same actor appeared in two or three places at once, boiled around for a while and then pulled himself together.

The trouble was, as it appeared later, that the company had lacked funds to buy its own equipment. The scenes had been shot by photographers hired by the day. One man had a Lumière camera, another had a Pathé and a third an Edison. Each camera used a different type of film. The perforations at the side of each strip of celluloid were spaced differently. The result was that at the first exhibition of the picture, the perforations, or sprocket holes, on the films did not fit the sprocket wheel of the projection machine. The sprocket might catch in one hole and miss the next three or four. Instead of moving uniformly, the film received a yank at irregular intervals, and between yanks it wriggled and twisted through the machine.

Goldwyn, Lasky and others rushed over to Philadelphia and laid the wreckage before Sig Lubin, who had a large film laboratory. The old-timer was enormously amused at the pathetic effort of the Broadway amateurs to break into his business. He had read some of Goldwyn's advertising literature which promised that the new company would revolutionize the industry. Lubin shook his head.

"Gentlemen, this is very grave," he said. After enjoying their terror for a while, he added, "But maybe it can be fixed."

"How long will it take?" asked Sam.

Lubin gazed jovially from one scared face to another. "I'll have it for you tomorrow," he said.

All that was necessary was to paste accurately spaced sprocket holes on the sides of the films. *The Squaw Man* was a tremendous hit. It did revolutionize the industry.

The Lasky company's second picture was *Brewster's Millions*. Its first private showing was another tragedy to Goldwyn and Lasky. *Brewster's Millions* was a wild farce. It unreeled to dead silence. The amateur magnates had forgotten that they were alone in the theater, and that it was necessary to have an audience to have gales of laughter. They were again sure they were ruined. "The films are no place for comedy," said Goldwyn. On the following morning *Brewster's Millions* was shown to a large audience of exhibitors. Goldwyn was too nervous to sit through it. He walked round and round the block, finally entering the theater about three minutes before the show was over. He was stunned to hear sounds of merriment. Adolph Zukor, head of Famous Players, congratulated his rivals.

Later Lasky said to Sam: "Zukor and all the other big fellows in the pictures smoke big cigars. Maybe we better."

Each bought a cigar and tried it. Lasky liked it and has smoked ever since. Sam got sick and never smoked another. He doesn't even smoke cigarettes, unless a duchess or countess presses one on him, and then he holds it like a fountain pen.

Lasky became active in the affairs of the company. This contradicted the old axiom that Goldwyn is boss. Terrific battles followed. After one combat Friend drove Sam around Central Park to cool him off. Central Park wasn't big enough for Sam's next rage. Friend drove him far down on Long Island.

"Why do you always fight?" asked Friend.

Goldwyn admitted that it came natural, but he shared the credit with Theodore Roosevelt. Sam had started reading the newspapers during the Big Stick days. He devoured T. R.'s fighting speeches.

"Theodore Roosevelt taught me that a man has to fight," said Sam.

"Yes, but you fight even when people agree with you," said Friend.

"Yes," said Goldwyn, "but Roosevelt teaches that the only things worth having are what you fight for."

There were further big rows in the Lasky company. Sam's associates became desperate. A meeting of De Mille, Lasky and Friend—three big, easy-going men—was held to oust Sam. Friend had the deciding vote.

"I'm willing," he said, "to vote Sam out, if you will promise to stick to it, but I won't vote him out today and then vote him back in tomorrow. I know he'll break your hearts and you'll vote him right back."

They voted Sam out. He was notified the following morning. Before night he had broken the hearts of Lasky and De Mille and was reinstated.

Both the Lasky company and Zukor's Famous Players were enormously successful. Zukor had the stars, but the Lasky company, largely because of De Mille, was the smartest picture maker. By bidding against each other for stars, they caused salaries to soar. Zukor, who was first in the field, had a property which, on paper, appeared twice as valuable as the Lasky company, but he was so eager to end competition that he offered a merger on a 50-50 basis. Before the legal agreement was complete, however, Zukor was as eager to get out of the merger as he had been to get into it. He had seen Sam in action. Once was enough. Zukor had ordered a contract drawn to pay Jack Pickford $500 a week; Sam howled and ordered the contract canceled. Zukor retired to his country estate, brooded for two days and handed in an ultimatum—either Sam must go or the merger must be canceled. Sam got out of the company, but he sold his stock for more than $900,000. Within less than three years after entering the pictures, he was approximately a millionaire.

Sam sold out late in 1916. He started immediately to organize a new company. He asked Edgar and Arch Selwyn, young Broadway producers, to join him. One of the assets of the Selwyns was their control of a library of plays some of which could be adapted to the movies. Edgar Selwyn was interested, but nervous, having heard of Sam's rows in the other company.

He went to Zukor and said: "Do you know any reason why I shouldn't go into business with Sam?"

Zukor studied for a while.

"As far as his honesty and integrity are concerned, there is none." Zukor studied again for a few moments and added, "But if you do, you'll be a most unhappy boy."

"Why?" asked Selwyn.

Zukor studied again. "Sam," he said finally, "is like a Jersey cow that gives the finest milk, but before you can take the bucket away, he has kicked it over."

The Selwyns notified Sam that they had decided not to go into business with him. But you can't do that to Sam. The Selwyns heard nothing for days except Sam's incantations. They held out until *rigor mortis* was about to set in, and then signed.

Sam's real name was Goldfish. The "Gold" was taken from Goldfish and the "wyn" from Selwyn, and they were combined to form the name of Goldwyn. The corporation was called Goldwyn Pictures Corporation. Sam's original Polish name had been slightly different, but on his arrival at Ellis Island the immigration officials had translated it as Goldfish. Sam saw nothing wrong with the name at that time. During his years as a glove cutter and glove salesman, the name caused him no mortification. When Sam stepped out into the amusement world, however, it was different. The name of Goldfish was made to order for Broadway wits. Sam could not have provoked more merriment if he wore a pigtail or a Lord Fauntleroy suit. On being introduced to Goldfish, you had to say something good or forfeit your reputation as a quick thinker. Sam arrived late one night at Ziegfeld's Midnight Frolic and was seated in the rear of the house behind a glass curtain which had been placed there to cut off a draft. Sam protested at being seated behind the glass. Gene Buck, Ziegfeld's associate, said, "Behind glass is the place for a Goldfish." Irvin S. Cobb's *Speaking of Operations* came out at about this time in the *Saturday Evening Post* with the goldfish simile which every educated American repeated several times a day. Sam finally went to his lawyer about it. The lawyer took it up with the New York Supreme Court and had Goldfish legally changed to Goldwyn. The Selwyns were furious at having half of their name pilfered, but they could do nothing about it. Thousands of corporations have been named after men, but Sam is one of the few men to be named after corporations.

There was a perverted sense of justice in Sam's change of name. For three years he had worked night and day in the other company to build up the name of Lasky. As soon as he had mastered the science of publicity, he regarded that as one of the major blunders of his life. His change of name squared the account; all the new company's publicity now had to glorify Sam personally. It was years, however, before Goldfish could get himself accepted as Goldwyn. Broadway resented the loss of so much sure-fire comedy. Sam is still occasionally addressed as "Mr. Goldfish." That is offering Sam the poisoned chalice. Disgruntled employees hold it out to the last.

As an embittered newspaperman looks forward to calling the managing editor a so-and-so, so the cankered Goldwyn employee looks forward to saying "Good-by, Mr. Goldfish."

In ousting Sam, the Zukor-Lasky group did not realize that they were creating a serious competitor. He was regarded as a good salesman, but as an ignoramus about picture making. In less than ten years, however, Goldwyn's new company was as great a factor in the movie business as the Zukor-Lasky combination. One of Sam's first steps had been to interest famous Broadway producers like Sam Harris, Arthur Hopkins and Al Woods. Sam has a certain amiable and attractive side when he wants to employ it. The combination of nuisance value and charm generally proved irresistible.

Sam was out to make great pictures, Goldwyn epics. He was willing to experiment and take chances. Arthur Hopkins made two suggestions for elevating the art, both of which were eagerly embraced by Goldwyn. The first was to have famous designers make the set. Hugo Ballin and Everett Shinn were engaged. A great improvement in the picture-making art resulted. The second Hopkins suggestion was to make films without subtitles, the action to be indicated so clearly that there would be no need to interrupt the flow of the picture for dialogue or verbal explanations. Hopkins was assigned to make *Fighting Odds,* a wordless picture. The idea excited all the salesmanship in Sam. If successful, it would give the new Goldwyn company a whirlwind start. When the all-pantomime film was partly made, theater owners were called in. Most of them thought their audiences would resent it. At the last minute the picture was filled with clumsy subtitles. The effect was disastrous.

Sam's greatest problem was that of finding stars. His rivals had contracts with nearly all the screen favorites. The first world celebrity to march under the Goldwyn banner was Maxine Elliott, who had had a twenty-year reign as the most beautiful woman on the stage. She was not the film type, however, and she had the bad luck to be the star of *Fighting Odds,* the ruined experiment in wordless pictures. The film was not only a failure in itself but it caused some exhibitors to cancel contracts for all future Goldwyn pictures. Sam's next effort to dethrone Mary Pickford and Theda Bara was his engagement of Mary Garden. She cost him $15,000 a week, and her *Thaïs* was a failure. Sam had supposed that Mary's prestige would sweep movie audiences off their feet, but he found that the movie public confused her with Mary Gardner, a heroine of the five-cent-picture days. Mary Garden is a great admirer of Goldwyn. "Sam and Oscar Hammerstein," she said, "are the two men you could trust without a contract." There was one consolation for Sam—Zukor and Lasky made a bigger mistake than he did. They tried to star Caruso as a romantic hero; on the silent screen he was just a 200-pound Neapolitan; the Caruso picture not only lost an enormous amount of cash but created a million dollars' worth of ill-will.

Sam has boundless courage, and is always at his best in disaster. He is unhappy and frightened when his affairs are prospering. Goldwyn hits alarm him; they inspire the fear that he and his whole staff will start resting on their oars. A famous director said, "I asked Sam how his Anna Sten picture was doing. His face lit up. He beamed and said, 'I'm losing my shirt.' I asked him about his Cantor picture. His jaw dropped and he became a picture of misery. He said, 'It'll make me a million.'"

Sam was at his happiest and best in 1918 when the sheriff's hot breath was always on his neck. He had invested huge sums in the wrong stars. The war had reduced theater attendance. In order to save coal, the Government had cut the commercial use of electric light, so that it was impracticable to make pictures at the Gold-

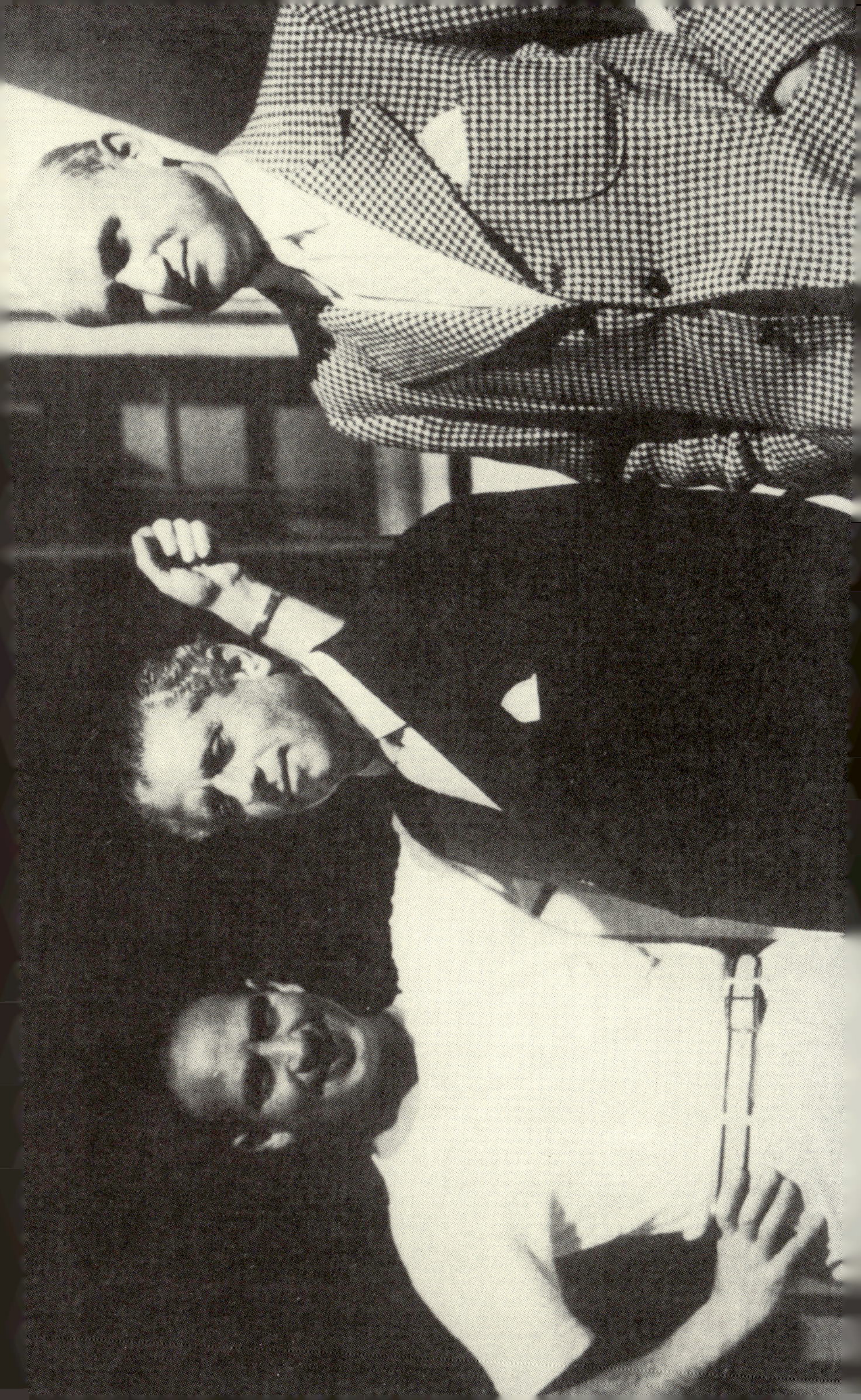

THREE MEN OF MOODS

Left to right: Harpo Marx, Max Reinhardt, Samuel Goldwyn.

wyn studio at Fort Lee, New Jersey. His competitors were using the free sunshine of Hollywood. Sam broke his ankle playing handball at the New York Athletic Club. He lay in a hospital bed with his injured leg in a hammock when a committee of his associates, including Al Woods, Arthur Hopkins, Sam Harris and Edgar Selwyn, called to tell him that bankruptcy was inevitable. Each told blacker news than the other. Sam sat propped up on the pillows, his fingertips pressed together. He beamed.

"Gentlemen," he said, "I see nothing but roses."

He met the week's pay roll by wiring his agencies to forward all cash on hand. Then he made some swift contacts with the Du Ponts and other sources of money. The armistice came in time to help him. Soon Sam was flourishing again. As he flourished, he became unhappy and began to squabble with his new associates. They got together and voted him out of his own company. Trouble made Sam less objectionable; they voted him back again.

After a merger, the Goldwyn company became Metro-Goldwyn-Mayer. Sam got out finally in 1923. There were some negotiations for his return. These, it was said, failed because Sam now wanted to change the name of Metro-Goldwyn-Mayer to Metro-Goldwyn-Mayer & Goldwyn. Sam started a third company in 1923, but he found himself in grave danger of losing his beautiful new name. Metro-Goldwyn-Mayer sued to prevent Sam from calling himself Goldwyn. A compromise was finally reached, permitting Sam to offer his pictures with the announcement, "Samuel Goldwyn Presents."

Goldwyn has a long record of "discoveries." Again and again he has made stars out of extras and bit players, but one young actress whom he failed to discover was Frances Howard. While Miss Howard was in her teens, Billie Burke took her to the Goldwyn studio in New York for a screen test. Sam saw the test. He called the head of the screen-test department upon the carpet. "Why," he demanded, "do you waste time and money this way?" Later Sam saw Miss Howard personally. The first time he ever spoke to her, he said, "You used to be fairly good-looking. Now that you've gone and bobbed your hair, you're terrible."

Sam was at that time campaigning against short hair. He felt so keenly on the subject that he once instructed his press department to cable to Rome and invite the Vatican to join him in his crusade against the bob. About a year after the screen test, Miss Howard made a hit on Broadway as the flapper in *The Best People*. She was hailed as one of the great beauties of the time. Paramount signed her and she made a screen hit as the star in *The*

Swan. Sam reversed himself. On April 23, 1925, he and Miss Howard were married at the City Hall, in Jersey City.

Just before they drove over to Jersey City, Miss Howard said, "Sam, there's a new magazine called *The New Yorker*. I hear it's clever. I wish you would get me a copy of it."

Sam got a copy. While waiting for his fiancée, he started reading it in his automobile. He was surprised to see his own picture. It was over an article which described Sam as the greatest man in Hollywood, a giant among pygmies. It credited him with imagination, infallible intuition, unlimited courage. Then it proceeded to explain Sam's greatness on the theory that he only had ten words in his vocabulary, most of them bad. A ten-word man, it argued, can always trample on the intellectuals, puzzled in their fogs of learning. On the other hand, it stated that five-word men could tower over and crush Sam with ease. In the course of some tributes to his artistic integrity, it said that an instinctive love of beauty was Sam's greatest trait next to acquisitiveness; also that he had once said to Edna Ferber, "I would rather make a great artistic picture than—than eat a good meal." Sam put the magazine away when Miss Howard entered the car; later he opened a window and pushed it out.

"What was that?" she asked.

He ignored the question and talked rapidly of other things.

"Did you get the magazine?" she asked.

"I forgot," said Sam.

He told people afterward that he was afraid she would break the engagement if she read it before the ceremony. "I learned later," said Sam, "that the article had been written by my press agent."

Sam had sworn Edgar Selwyn, his best man, to secrecy about the wedding.

"Why?" asked Selwyn.

"I don't want any publicity," said Sam.

"You don't want any publicity!" said Selwyn.

"No," said Sam, "I don't want any publicity."

Selwyn had never before known Sam to make any anti-publicity arrangements; it was like Dexter Fellows asking people to make a confidential matter of the circus. Selwyn kept the secret, but he didn't think Sam would. There were mobs of newspapermen at the wedding. Sam posed relentlessly for the photographers and scraped conversations indefatigably with the reporters.

"I thought you didn't want any publicity," said Selwyn.

"Can I control the press?" inquired Goldwyn.

3

GOLDWYN HAS ALWAYS HAD A PASSION FOR quality. When he was a nineteen-year-old glove salesman, he tried to organize a company to manufacture gloves of unparalleled quality. The plan collapsed because the financial backer withdrew on learning that Sam was a minor and could not be bound by a contract.

"Quality" pictures were Sam's aim when he entered the films in 1913, and he was a leading factor in the change from the Wild West thrillers and the white-slave shockers to the modern feature picture. In 1919, Sam wanted to elevate the pictures again. For several years he had had the idea that the writer should be the key man in the pictures; that the scenario or script should be something better than a rough draft for a director to follow or throw away, as he saw fit. Sam had an inspiration; he would corner the world supply of literary artists; all great writers would be Goldwyn writers.

In his enthusiasm, Sam thought that he might be able to advertise the names of the writers in big lights and the names of the stars in small lights. If the movie public accepted this, it would solve Sam's problem. When he broke away from Zukor and Lasky in 1916, and founded his own company, Goldwyn's great difficulty was that of finding stars. His competitors had most of the popular favorites under contract. If Sam could make the public more excited over Gertrude Atherton than Mary Pickford or wilder over Gouverneur Morris than Douglas Fairbanks, the Goldwyn company would lead the field.

Sam organized The Eminent Authors Inc. His first consignment of genius to arrive in Hollywood included Rex Beach, Rupert Hughes, Mary Roberts Rinehart, Gertrude Atherton, Basil King, Gouverneur Morris and Leroy Scott. Sam's new move frightened his competitors. They doubted if men of letters would become great box-office stars, but they wanted to be protected. Sam had cleaned up the home market so thoroughly that his rivals had to import Elinor Glyn, Sir Gilbert

Parker, Somerset Maugham, Arnold Bennett and others. Ordinary writers were weeded out of the studios to make room for famous authors. One of the ousted scenarists was Darryl F. Zanuck, now chief of Twentieth Century-Fox, who was reduced to working in a shipyard.

For a time the heaviest duty of Sam's eminent authors was that of being photographed in the act of gazing admiringly at Sam. When they started to write for the pictures, the results were not uniform.

Sam read the first work of Leroy Scott and said: "Mr. Scott, you are undoubtedly the greatest writer in the world, but maybe this is not good for the movies."

When he read the first scenario by Basil King, Sam said, "Mr. King, you are undoubtedly the greatest writer in the world, but maybe this is not good for the movies."

Every Goldwyn author was told that he was undoubtedly the greatest writer in the world, and so on. The venture was not wholly a failure, however. Sam got his money's worth in publicity, and Rupert Hughes wrote the script of *The Old Nest*, which drew more than a million dollars at the box office.

Sam wanted to make a Goldwyn writer of George Bernard Shaw. They discussed it over tea one day in London. Shaw thought Sam was too esthetic to be a practical man. A version of the conversation was cabled over to Howard Dietz, Goldwyn's publicity chief; he compressed Shaw's words into: "The trouble, Mr. Goldwyn, is that you are only interested in art and I am only interested in money." This was cabled back to London and released there. It added considerably to Shaw's reputation as a wit.

The most eminent of Goldwyn's Eminent Authors was Maurice Maeterlinck. The great Belgian poet had come to the United States shortly after the war for a lecture tour. His first appearance was at Carnegie Hall. Maeterlinck spoke no English. He wrote the lecture in French and had it translated literally into English. Then he had each English syllable retranslated into a French syllable. Each English sound was to be rendered by an approximate French sound. The result was a lecture in mispronounced anagrams. Delivered to a Franco-American audience, it was equally unintelligible to the French and to the Americans. It was a new literary form; it was not even nonsense, so it topped Gertrude Stein.

The lecture caused the cancellation of the rest of the lecture tour. Maeterlinck was free, and Sam went after him. Since his words had to be translated, Sam was shorn of half of his sales craft; his gestures and grimaces failed to synchronize with his selling points. Thus handicapped, Sam made slow progress. He thought the poet's weakness was vanity, and he tried to play on this infirmity by explaining what it meant to Maeterlinck to get to be a Goldwyn writer; how proud the folks back home would be. Sam made a success story of it—a rookie becoming a big-league star overnight. Maeterlinck looked blank. Sam tried again to fire the man's ambition; "You'll get equal treatment with Rex Beach," he said. Maeterlinck still had an expression of bewilderment which Sam took for an expression of incredulity. Sam ordered all the contracts with eminent authors to be brought in.

"You're getting as much money as any of them," said Sam. To verify this, he handed the Basil King contract to Maeterlinck.

"You know Basil King?" said Sam.

This was translated to Maeterlinck, who said: *"Non."*

Other contracts were handed to the Belgian, and other questions translated by the interpreter.

"You know Rupert Hughes?"

"Non."

"Mary Roberts Rinehart?"

"Non."

"Rex Beach?"

"*Non.*"

Sam went down the list, getting a "*Non*" at each name.

He turned to his press agent and whispered: "What's the matter with this guy? Is he dumb?"

Maeterlinck understood five figures, however, and he joined the Goldwyn literary colony. The private car which had been used by Woodrow Wilson when he stumped the country for the League of Nations was obtained by Howard Dietz, the publicity chief, for Maeterlinck's trip from New York to Hollywood. A publicity man was placed on the car to issue, at every stop, statements by Maeterlinck glorifying America and Goldwyn.

America was eager to hear from the poet. The Blue Bird craze started by Maeterlinck's play was fresh in the public mind. The publicity scheme was a disappointment, however, to Dietz and Goldwyn. One member of the party in the private car was Maeterlinck's lecture manager. Maeterlinck would soon pick up enough English to make a million-dollar lecture tour of America, according to the manager's reasoning, and he had a contract for a percentage of the receipts. He reasoned further that, if Maeterlinck gave away a lot of words now, he would not be able to sell them later. To the lecture manager, every Maeterlinck statement to the press today meant a hundred empty seats sometime in the future. The entire journey was a battle between the publicity man and the lecture manager, the poet siding with the lecture manager, who wore a frock coat and called him "Master." For hundreds of miles at a stretch, the Maeterlinck special got less publicity than a cattle train.

Goldwyn's representative at Dallas was a go-getting Texan named Lew Remy. He arranged a banquet there for Maeterlinck. The mayor of Dallas, the governor of Texas and all the leading citizens of the Southwest came. The banquet was a disappointment. The great Belgian did not arrive. The lecture manager had rerouted the private car and made it miss Dallas entirely. Lew Remy learned the new route that the Maeterlinck party was taking, and wired to a Texas friend at another town to meet the train and page the lecture manager. "Then punch him in the nose," concluded Remy's message. The lecture manager was duly paged.

"Are you Mr. —— ?" asked Remy's friend.

"I am," said the manager.

Instantly he was stretched out flat on the platform.

Arriving finally at Hollywood, Maeterlinck demanded a house on a hilltop, so that he could see the sun better. That was provided. There are witnesses in Hollywood who will sign affidavits that Maeterlinck's first effort was a film adaptation of his *Life of a Bee,* and that, on reading it, Goldwyn ran out screaming, "My God, the hero is a bee!" Goldwyn's own recollection is that Maeterlinck's first scenario was about a little boy and a mattress and a lot of blue feathers.

In order to saturate the poet in Hollywood psychology, he was then taken, day after day, to projection rooms to see action pictures. His next scenario started with the lid slowly rising from a sewer in a street of Paris; up from the sewer came the face of a gory and bedraggled female Apache with a dagger gripped between her teeth. Maeterlinck's Hollywood writings were not made into pictures. It is said that, when Maeterlinck left Hollywood, Goldwyn saw him to the station, patted him on the shoulder and said, "Don't worry, Maurice. You'll make good yet."

Maeterlinck was at Cannes a year ago when Goldwyn was there with Lord Beaverbrook; Sam was asked if he wanted to meet Maeterlinck; "No," he said, "I saw enough of that man years ago."

In spite of his experiences with Maeterlinck and certain other members of Eminent Authors Pictures, Inc., Goldwyn always stuck to his theory that the writers were the most important people in the pictures. Goldwyn is king, but writers are those nearest the throne. Sam will go anywhere, do anything, to sign a man he thinks is a great writer. To some extent he has suffered because of his worship of letters. For nearly a quarter of a century he has surrounded himself with crack novelists and playwrights. They studied Goldwyn as a strange zoological specimen. They treasured his curious sayings and constantly added to the Goldwyn legend. Some intimates of Sam assert that he does not make any more breaks in English than any other man who was not reared by a governess, but that Sam's breaks are always caught and preserved. Except for years of close association with writers, Goldwyn would not be known today as a surrealist word painter and master of the misspoken word. On the other hand, Sam has benefited by his association with writers. He can be articulate when he abandons his mind to it; much of the time, however, he is struggling with ideas and lets expression take care of itself. Sam may be lucky that his English education consisted only of one year at night school; his power seems to consist in a simplicity and elemental directness of mind which does not always flourish under higher education. There was not even a dictionary at the night school that Sam attended. He was astonished at the enormous size of a volume which was brought forth at a Hollywood party to be consulted at the game of Guggenheim.

"What a big book!" said Sam. "Who wrote it?"

"Webster," was the reply.

"It must have taken him a long time."

"About a century."

"My, my!" said Sam. "Fifty years!"

Sam laid no claim to being an artist when he organized the Lasky company in 1913. He was the salesman and businessman of the company. When he organized his own company in 1916, he was everything. He found that he had to do his own editing and cutting in order to keep studio politics and studio amours out of the pictures. Some of the directors were more intent on their own romances than on those of the pictures; close-ups and other scenes were sometimes slipped in for reasons not connected with the plot. Salesmanship was Goldwyn's specialty, and he found that he ought to know all about his pictures in order to sell them.

For example, after the war Sam saw a chance to invade England, so he looked for pictures that he could sell to the British public. Among others he made *Lord and Lady Algy* and *The Gay Lord Quex*. He went abroad to sell them. One of his cables home was, "I went to see Lord and Lady Algy three nights ago and I am still sick." Sam insisted on better pictures, so that he could sell them better. He absorbed picture knowledge rapidly and developed into one of the shrewdest judges of story values.

Sam's competitors were slow in admitting his talent as a producer, but they venerated him as a salesman, showman and publicity man. He has always been considered unequalled at stirring up excitement about his forthcoming pictures. Theater owners bleated about Sam's prices, but they nearly all paid them. One of Sam's rare defeats in a duel between buyer and seller was inflicted on him by the late Abraham Finkelstein, of Minneapolis. Salesmen reported that Finkelstein was obdurate; he positively refused to buy a Goldwyn picture at the price asked. Sam gave the agent an inspirational talk by telephone; the agent tackled Finkelstein again, but failed again. "I'll go there myself and show you how to sell pictures," said Sam.

He was off for Minneapolis. Finkelstein, a tall, elderly, stoop-shouldered man, listened to Sam with grave courtesy until Sam named the price; then he pressed a buzzer. Two men in the uniforms of lunatic-asylum attendants came in and led Sam out. Sam came back later and announced that he would build a theater in Minneapolis and run Finkelstein out of business. Finkelstein reached for his hat and coat. "Come with me," he said, "and I'll show you the best sites." He drove Sam around town, pointing out the good locations for movie palaces, but Sam didn't build.

Sam's love of publicity for the name of Goldwyn has been attributed to egotism. This theory is not utterly fantastic. Sam does not try to conceal the fact that he has an ego. In a word battle with Herman Shumlin, the Broadway producer, Sam could think of nothing more withering to say than "You're a bigger egotist than I am." Publicity for the name of Goldwyn, however, is important in salesmanship. The public may not be stampeded into picture houses by the mere name of Goldwyn, but the name does mean something to proprietors and managers of motion-picture houses. If Sam made inferior pictures, his personal publicity would be injurious to him. His name would be associated in the minds of exhibitors with vacant seats and red ink. While Sam steadily produces superior pictures, his personal publicity is an important department of salesmanship. Sam has had many of the best press agents in the country, but they have never got enough publicity to satisfy him for long. Pete Smith, now the famous Voice of the Films, was a Goldwyn press agent. He did satisfy Sam once for two or three days by a publicity coup.

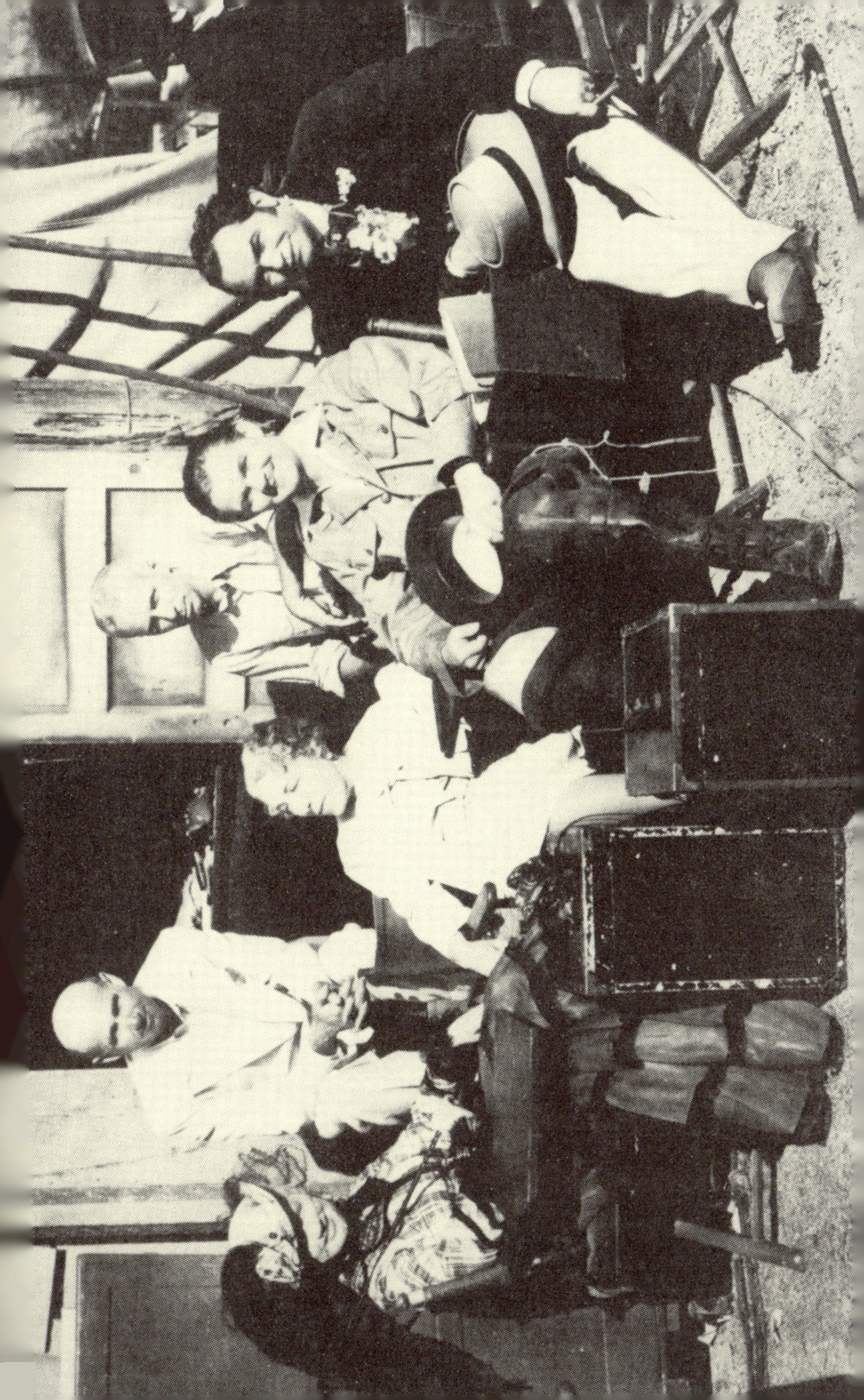

TIME OUT ON THE SET

This picture was taken during the filming of "Barbary Coast" in 1935. Left to right: Miriam Hopkins, Mr. Goldwyn, Edna Ferber, Howard Hawks, Lawrence Tibbett, Edward G. Robinson.

THE GREAT GOLDWYN

Pete Smith proposed the idea that Sam should get himself talked about by announcing that there were only thirteen real actors in Hollywood and naming them. Sam was afraid at first; he thought it would create thirteen ingrates and a thousand enemies. Finally Sam had a stroke of genius himself; he said, "I'll name twelve and say the thirteenth is a mystery, and every actor and actress in Hollywood will think he's the mystery." It made a sensation, and Sam followed it up next day with a column discussing possible entries for the thirteenth place.

Sam was abroad part of the time while Pete Smith was his press agent. He returned to Hollywood full of enthusiasm. Laying some large photographs of himself before the press agent, Sam said: "What do you think of those?"

"All right," said Smith.

"Only all right?" inquired Sam.

"They do justice to you," said Smith. "They look as if they would reproduce all right."

"Pete, I'm disappointed in you," said Goldwyn. "Don't you see they're eleven by fourteen inches? They're too big for the newspapers to put in one column. Don't you grasp the idea? From now on they'll have to print my picture in two columns."

The publicity man broke his employer's heart by explaining that newspapers could take a photograph as big as a billboard and reduce it to a one-column cut. Pete Smith, like some other hard-boiled publicity men who worked for Goldwyn, did not take him too seriously, and put up with his tantrums as long as he paid well.

Sam had a love of being met by impressive turnouts on his arrival from New York or Europe. Smith managed to get a couple of bona-fide news photographers down to the train, and then padded out the camera battalion by calling on personal friends to show up at the station with cameras.

Sam, always a tremendous walker, used to make Smith walk with him in the mornings from the Goldwyn home to the Goldwyn studio, a distance of four or five miles. One morning Sam saw a rival's advertising banner stretched across Beverly Boulevard.

"That's good advertising," said Sam. "That's what I want for our première. Only instead of one banner, I want hundreds—one on every corner, all the way to the theater."

Smith saw that the banner stretched across the street between two pieces of property owned by the rival company. He could see that Goldwyn's idea of hundreds of banners would mean hundreds of negotiations with property owners. Furthermore, there was a city ordinance against such banners. He knew, however, that opposition would only make Sam rabid in favor of the idea. His only escape from an impossible task was to make a bad argument in favor of it.

He estimated that the banners would cost about fifteen dollars apiece, and he said: "That's a great scheme. Those banners will only cost a hundred and fifty or a hundred and seventy-five dollars apiece. We can put up two hundred of them for about thirty thousand dollars, or more if you like."

It ended with Goldwyn rebuking Smith for having such an expensive and mediocre idea.

The Goldwyn publicity department is a sort of public-health department at times. The streak of the absolute monarch in Sam inspires him with real anxiety for the health of all the potentates of the earth. He is said to identify himself with them so closely that when one is sick, Sam goes on a diet; when one dies, Sam feels that his own time has come.

He is like a certain Princess of Tarente, who put on mourning whenever a member of any royal house died in any part of Europe. On one occasion she did appear in brilliant colors; Madame de Sévigné said, "Madame, I rejoice in the health of Europe." Similarly, if Sam is gay, it means there are not likely to be any big obituaries in the paper tomorrow. He does at times worry about other than the top personalities. One Saturday afternoon he met a studio executive who seemed seriously stricken. "You look all run down," said Sam. "Go home. Don't come back till Monday morning." Sam was discovered one day in distress. He had before him a letter telling him not to send any more money to an aged woman living in New York, because she had died; she had been Sam's first landlady when he arrived in New York as a boy, and had fed and lodged him when he was broke. Another streak of humanity asserted itself in Goldwyn once when he recognized an extra on one of his sets. "Come away quick," he said to his studio manager. The extra had once been a Goldwyn star; she had quarreled with him, had become a free lance and had bad luck. "I didn't want her to see me," said Goldwyn. "It would embarrass her." His chief anxiety, however, is for great people.

He called up his press agent one morning and asked: "How is the President?"

"Fine," said the press agent. "I was with him last night and he was fine."

"What do you mean, you were with him last night?"

"Mr. Schenck and I were together last night," said

the press agent, referring to Joseph Schenck, president of United Artists.

"No, no," said Goldwyn. "I mean Roosevelt. The paper says he has a cold. Find out how he is and let me know at once."

The press agent telephoned to a friend on the United Press and found out the President was all right. He then telephoned to Goldwyn and said: "I had the UP carry a special wire to the White House saying Mr. Goldwyn was anxious to know how the President was this morning, and the President thanks Mr. Goldwyn for his kindness and says that he is feeling much better."

"That's the kind of service I like," said Goldwyn. He was satisfied with the press agent for hours.

As Pete Smith used to pad the welcoming camera batteries with dummies, another press agent used to upholster the Goldwyn interviews with fraudulent interrogators. Two or three local reporters would be present. In addition, the publicity man would call in eight or ten reliable pals who would be presented to Goldwyn as "Mr. Wolgast, of the Chicago Tribune, Mr. Berlenbach, of the New York Times, Mr. Greb, of the London Daily News," and so on. Devices of this kind, however, were only used when it was considered important to put on a special show. The Goldwyn publicity man's brain is usually working with great rapidity in the interest of getting big displays in newspapers and magazines. Goldwyn men have to have their hearts in the cause.

There has always been an argument among Goldwyn scholars as to whether his rages are genuine, or part of a routine. Sam is an old head salesman both in gloves and pictures. A head salesman's business is to scourge the soul of the junior salesman in order to fill him with enterprise. You blast his morale, accuse him of wrongfully cumbering the earth and cheating potter's field, and then send him forth to overwhelm the customers with his victorious personality. However, Goldwyn does not discriminate in favor of his own subordinates in his rages and furies; he has had shouting affrays with nearly all the big figures in the industry, and when he lets go there is not a word in or out of the language that he hesitates to use. The theory that his tornadoes are artificial is based on the fact that he can turn off the ferocity and turn on the charm in an instant. He has no hangover from one mood to another. An outburst that might leave another man sick for days is completely out of Sam's system the moment the uproar is over. He is too busy to waste time in the transition from one emotional state to another. A split second separates Ivan the Terrible from Mr. Pickwick.

THE GREAT GOLDWYN

One day Sam blazed away at his current press chief, Jock Lawrence, most of the afternoon. After going to bed that night, Sam summoned the press agent and started blazing away again. Samuel Goldwyn, Jr., then a boy of seven or eight, entered the room to say good night to his father. Sam's fist stopped in mid-air; he beamed; he chatted gaily about school problems; at last he tenderly advised his son to run along and get plenty of sleep.

As the boy was leaving the room, Sam made a genial gesture in the direction of Jock Lawrence and cooed: "Kiss Uncle Jock good night."

The boy obeyed and left.

"And furthermore ——" resumed Sam, furiously addressing the publicity man, starting to rail at him again from the precise point at which he had been interrupted by the entrance of Sam, Jr.

Sam thinks so fast that the latter end of his argument sometimes refutes the beginning.

"I have never had a lawsuit in my career," he said. "That shows you that I'm easy to get along with. I'm the most reasonable man out here. I've never had a lawsuit worth mentioning. Three or four, maybe. Right now I'm being sued by Paramount for five million dollars. It's one of the most important lawsuits in the country."

He started a speech to salesmen once by telling them

to be reasonable with theater owners, some of whom had complained of being gouged. He asked the salesmen to be very moderate in their demands. But in his peroration the old sales instinct seized him, and he exhorted them to go after the last cent. The final line of his speech is generally quoted. "This business is dog eat dog, and nobody is going to eat me."

He complained by telephone because another studio had borrowed a Goldwyn writer for a few hours without his permission. Sam was told that every effort had been made to get in touch with him, and that it was finally assumed that he would have been agreeable.

Sam kept repeating: "If you only had the decency to ask me."

"What would you have said, Mr. Goldwyn?"

"I would have said 'No,'" replied Sam.

Sam fears contentment. He has seen contentment ruin many of the great figures in the industry. He is afraid of making the people around him contented; that is one cause of his being more liberal with blame than with praise. A press agent once wanted to resign; one reason was that Goldwyn had never said a good word about his work. "If I don't say it's bad, it's good," said Sam. He hates yes men; he loves no men, but he is fond of having no men answer him in the affirmative. This becomes com-

THE GREAT GOLDWYN

plicated. Sam once became greatly smitten with a Hollywood executive noted for his rugged way of saying no. Sam hired him at an enormous salary; the man turned out to be a yes man; he could say no to others, but not to the furious Goldwyn. The contract expired; the employee was held over on a weekly salary to finish a job; no longer in awe of Sam, he was able to say, "It stinks. ... It's awful. ... It's gruesome," and so on. Sam, impressed, put him under contract again; the man again started saying, "It's fine. ... It's great. ... It's wonderful," and was useless again.

Sam is at his best when talking to one person. He is a tête-à-tête evangelist. His man-to-man conferences become rousing revivals or camp meetings, and usually end with the party of the second part on the mourner's bench, putting his signature on a contract. The day before his death last January, Richard Boleslawski, the derector, said that one of his most memorable experiences was a talk with Goldwyn.

"My book, *The Way of a Lancer*, had just come out," he said. "Sam called me over in great haste and wanted to buy it then and there. I told him there were two other interested parties and that I couldn't sell it without their permission. He handed me two telephones and said, 'Get them.' I got one in New York and one in Ohio. Sam battled with them over the price, but a good stiff one was finally agreed on. 'We'll sign right now,' said Sam, putting five hundred dollars option money in my hand. I said I thought I ought to see my lawyer. He put his arm around me and said, 'I'll be your lawyer.' I tried to argue, but he hypnotized me. There was no standing up against his impetuosity. He drew up the contract and I signed it. Later he changed his mind and didn't want to make *The Way of a Lancer*. I thought the contract called for the amount agreed on, but it only called for the five hundred dollars option money. I never felt that Sam intended to take advantage, but I thought I would have been better advised to see a lawyer. That was my only personal contact with him, but I am one of his greatest admirers. He has a real and spontaneous love of beauty. He hates the phony and will do anything to get the real thing."

4

THE ONLY PROLONGED VACATION THAT GOLDwyn ever took during his movie career was in 1923. It was an involuntary one. Sam had been defeated in a battle for control of Metro-Goldwyn-Mayer. The head of the anti-Goldwyn faction was the late Joe Godsol. The hate between Joe and Sam was satanic. Godsol was not satisfied with taking Sam's company away from him. In an effort to inflict the greatest possible humiliation on Sam, Joe took to studying maps. He picked out a remote hamlet in Canada. He issued a peremptory order to Sam to proceed forthwith to this frontier post, establish an M-G-M office there and take charge of it.

In order to enjoy his revenge to the full, Godsol had

spies watch Sam and see how he took it. Sam was a disappointment. His everyday rages were so terrific that he could not improve on them. Sam appreciated the insult; he, a founder of the two greatest companies in the pictures, ordered to the region of perpetual snows; but he had developed his routine frenzy to such a point that he could not top it on a special occasion.

Instead of going to Canada, Sam took a house at Great Neck, Long Island, and started to take it easy while lawyers adjusted his affairs with M-G-M. Arthur Hammerstein, the Broadway producer, shared the Great Neck house with Sam.

One day Goldwyn arrived at Great Neck, dusty and abnormally indignant. "I'm going to have that chauffeur arrested," he said. Before his row with M-G-M, Sam had bossed thousands; since then he had only had his driver to boss. Sam did not know how to operate a car himself, but he was outraged by every move the driver made. For days the man was the exclusive recipient of the anger which Goldwyn had normally distributed among multitudes. Finally he drove Goldwyn to a lonely spot on the Jericho Turnpike in the most deserted section of Long Island. He stopped the car and got out. "I'm quitting," he said, and walked rapidly off. Goldwyn had to tramp for miles to find a man to drive him home.

THE GREAT GOLDWYN

While he was marking time at Great Neck, Goldwyn started to dictate his memoirs. Sam's prose at that time was not up to his later standard. Hammerstein asked, "Who's going to translate it for you?" It was entitled, *Behind the Screen*. Sam sold the book, magazine, serial and other rights to it for more than $100,000. The book complimented everybody in the pictures except Godsol. Between stretches of dictation, Sam learned to swim at the Great Neck beach. Even Sam's paddling in Long Island Sound was done in royal Goldwyn manner. He was always going too far out and being rescued. Sam was the sovereign; all others his faithful liege men. He risked drowning because he felt sure that a retinue of his faithful subjects would always be at hand to save him.

Sam's long vacation ended after he had sold his interest in M-G-M for a big price. He now founded a new company, Samuel Goldwyn, Inc., Ltd. After his experiences with associates, directors and stockholders, Sam decided to have nothing further to do with them, and for the last fourteen years he has been absolute within his own domain. His former companies are great organizations, each of which turns out forty-five or fifty pictures a year. Goldwyn is content to make only eight or nine, but he works over every detail of these. He has vetoed all proposals to expand by selling stock to the public or

THE GREAT GOLDWYN

by taking in partners. "I found," he said, "that it took a world of time to explain my plans to my associates; now I can save all that time and energy, and put it into making better pictures."

Sam has become more important since he started to go it alone and to make a comparatively small number of pictures annually. His former associates rubbed their eyes twelve years ago when he made *Stella Dallas*. When he followed this with *The Dark Angel*, it had to be admitted that *Stella Dallas* was no accident. Sam had to be a pacemaker in quality. As an independent competing with the big factories of Hollywood and the large theater chains, he had to make superior pictures or quit.

Goldwyn prides himself on looking ahead and reading the future. He has a good record as a prophet. When the talking picture came in, a decade ago, he saw that it would revolutionize love. The needle hiss, the frying sound and other incidental noises of the early apparatus spoiled the tender sequences. Audiences which used to pant at the prolonged clinches and three-minute kisses went into hysterics. The sweethearts of the early talkies were inclined to lisp or croak. John Gilbert and other important heartbreakers were whistled off the screen because their love talk was a mixture of guttural and falsetto. Ronald Colman, a Goldwyn star, was saved from this. Sam would not let Colman carry on a courtship or even a flirtation in the presence of the primitive microphone which caused a lover to low like a young bull calf. He took the star out of romance and put him into melodrama, and Colman maintained his prestige. There was no serious billing and cooing in Goldwyn pictures until the sound apparatus stopped making Romeos sound like barnyard imitators.

Sam was one of the first to realize that dialogue was to be far more important in the talkies than subtitles had been in the silent pictures. One great director of that time had said, "We don't need anybody to write dialogue. Just put the actors into the situations and let them say what pops into their minds." It was discovered that this did not work. It was also discovered that the writing of dialogue was different from the writing of subtitles. The ear was found to be more critical than the eye. The conversation, or subtitles, of the silent days could be naïve or maudlin or bombastic without irritating the eye, but the ear was less tolerant. It was found to rebel against phony effects. Goldwyn had always regarded motion pictures as a branch of the writing trade; it was natural for him to foresee that the writer would now be supreme; he immediately sought some of the leading playwrights of the country to write his dialogue. The early

THE GREAT GOLDWYN

Goldwyn pictures were highly finished products compared to most of the others.

The new medium baffled Goldwyn in one respect. It made music an important factor in pictures. By instinct and experience, Sam knew nearly everything else about his art; he was able to put "the Goldwyn touch" on costumes, settings, character, dialogue and plot construction, but he did not know music. Sam's competitors were no better off than he was. Most of the magnates and executives grappled resolutely with the new subject and became music masters in no time. As Al Newman, a Hollywood musical director, said, "Everybody here knows his business, plus music." By his talent for picking the right people, Sam has made successful musical shows, but he has not been able to Goldwynize his music. He cannot, as yet, give composers and song writers the same sure guidance that he bestows on other employees.

Sam has developed a musical vocabulary of his own. When he made his first musical picture, he heard one-step time described as two-four time. He translated the phrase as "two-by-four time." Sam told a composer once that his music would not do.

"What's the matter with it?" asked the composer.

"There's not enough sarcasm in it," said Sam.

More recently Sam became enthusiastic about the song,

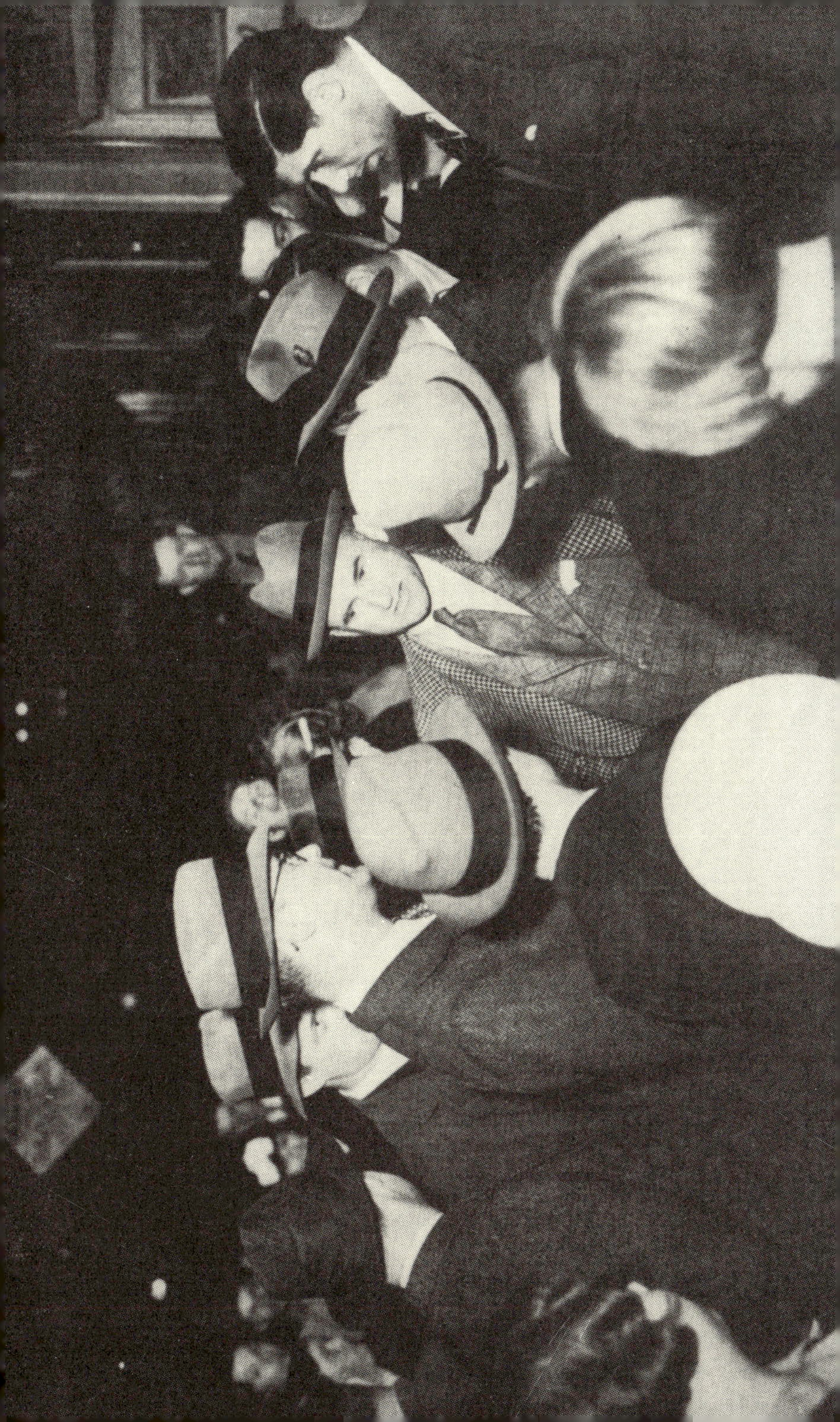

AFTER A PREVIEW

Mr. Goldwyn, surrounded by members of his executive staff, discusses the audience reaction to a new Goldwyn production after a "sneak preview" at a Hollywood neighborhood theatre.

Night and Day. "We must have something like Night and Day for our new show," he kept insisting. One man dined at the Goldwyn home after hearing Sam rave all afternoon about Night and Day. After dinner, Night and Day was played on the phonograph. "What tune is that?" asked Sam.

Goldwyn wanted the Easter music exactly right for a Greek Orthodox church service in the picture, *We Live Again*, based on Tolstoy's *Resurrection*. He was in ecstasies when the service was played for him privately in the studio auditorium. Sam rushed around the lot, calling important executives away from their work to hear it. The music had been recorded on a film. Someone had forgotten to rewind it. At the second demonstration, the film began to move in the wrong direction, and the music was being played backwards. The technician detected the error and was about to correct it, when he heard murmurs of "Great" . . . "Magnificent." The thing had now gone too far; the technical man was afraid of getting into trouble, and he let the music continue in the reverse. The entire Greek Orthodox Easter service was played backwards, and at the end the auditorium rang with applause.

Sam is an autocrat. He cannot stand an equal or superior in authority. But as long as his final say cannot be questioned, he is a glutton for suggestions. He goes around begging for criticism and advice. He is not inventive or creative. He occasionally gets an idea of his own, but even if he regards it as a stroke of genius he can be persuaded to give it up. In one of his pictures, Sam was having difficulty in finding a smooth transition from a black-and-white sequence to a color sequence. A solution was finally discovered; immediately afterward, Sam thought of a different solution. He called his advisers together, laid the new thought before them and asked their opinions.

"We have spent weeks straightening the thing out, and this would throw it back into confusion," said one. Three others were equally hostile.

The fifth said: "I don't know if I understood you correctly, but if I did, it stinks."

"I can get a bad idea," said Sam.

Goldwyn hates to share power. He finds it equally objectionable to share glory. For years his head man was Arthur Hornblow, Jr. Sam had, and still has, a high respect for him. They parted because Hornblow wanted credit; he wanted a mention on the screen in pictures made largely by him. Sam's reaction to this was like that of Henry IV when he caught the Prince of Wales trying on the crown; he was wounded to the heart. The fact that Hornblow was entitled to screen credit, by all the canons of Hollywood, did not affect Sam. He was ready to give more money, European vacations, or anything except participation in the Goldwyn fame.

The nearest that Sam came to dividing glory was his signing of Flo Ziegfeld in 1930 to help in making *Whoopee*, Sam's first talkie. As a partner, Ziegfeld would have been unbearable to Sam; as an employee he was highly acceptable. Sam listened humbly to the Great Ziegfeld; but when decisions were made, the Great Goldwyn made them. One of the triumphs of Sam's career was the fact that Ziegfeld, in leaving Hollywood, carried off a troupe of Goldwyn girls with him and presented them to Broadway as Ziegfeld girls. Ziegfeld had been delayed in going to Hollywood to help make *Whoopee*. Goldwyn picked his own chorus. "They're terrible, impossible," said Ziegfeld. Everyone was greatly impressed except Goldwyn. He looked on himself as a judge of beauty, and doubted if Ziegfeld could top his selections. Ziegfeld went back to New York and brought back two dozen Ziegfeld girls. The rival choruses were placed on display. "You win," said Ziegfeld rather magnificently. His chorus was shipped back to New York. After *Whoopee* had been completed, Ziegfeld signed up most of the Goldwyn girls. Among them were Virginia

Bruce, Barbara Weeks, Marian Marsh and Paulette Goddard.

Will Rogers was one of Sam's first "discoveries." His first picture was made for Sam in 1919; for several years he appeared exclusively in Goldwyn comedies. In a single picture, *Stella Dallas*, Goldwyn raised Belle Bennett and Lois Moran from obscurity to stardom. The most important of the Goldwyn finds was Vilma Banky. Sam discovered Gary Cooper when Gary was a cowboy, but he failed to appreciate Cooper after discovering him. Ten years ago, Sam was paying Cooper fifty dollars a week; he generously released Cooper when the young actor got an offer of $200 a week; recently Goldwyn re-hired Cooper for $3000 a week. He regards his failure to develop Cooper in the first place as one of the major blunders of his career. Robert Montgomery is another Goldwyn discovery. Screen tests were made of Montgomery when he was an actor on Broadway. "His neck is too long," was the report. Sam saw the tests and said. "His neck is not too long; his collars are too short." He wired his office in New York to ask Arthur Richman, playwright and connoisseur of clothes, to have neck-correcting shirts made for Montgomery. New screen tests were made; the actor looked great in his inspired haberdashery. Through another man's mistake, Goldwyn did not get the benefit of this discovery. On the strength of the revised screen test, Montgomery was signed by M-G-M.

Of all Goldwyn's discoveries, the costliest was Anna Sten. Goldwyn brought Miss Sten to this country from Poland, after seeing her in a European film. He paid her a large salary for a year while English teachers and dramatic coaches worked on her. He would not listen to adverse judgments of her. She had, in his opinion, the enigmatic countenance of the Sphinx. He went around telling everyone, "She has the face of a Spink." In addition to the mysterious beauty which he saw in her, he said she was a great actress, and also a singer and dancer. He was disillusioned on the last two points. After hearing her sing, a vocal expert reported, "She has a small but highly disagreeable voice." Her limitations as a dancer were such that, in rehearsing for *Nana*, Goldwyn himself hopped around on his left foot and tried to wrap his right leg around his neck, in an effort to teach her to cancan. She had a husband who was full of ideas which greatly differed from Goldwyn's. Sam signed the husband as an assistant director and sent him away to Catalina Island to work on another picture; but still Miss Sten was a problem. When Sam spent $411,000 on *Nana*, he scrapped everything that had been done and started all over.

The morale of the studio broke under the terrific grind of imprinting the Goldwyn touch on Miss Sten. Nervous wrecks directed nervous wrecks. One day Miss Sten collapsed. "Brandy," cried Goldwyn. Work was resumed, but there were more collapses and more cries for restoratives. On one scene was a gorgeous bed with carved swans and doves, the dream bed of the Nanas of all time. Between scenes, Miss Sten rested on it.

Standing on a platform near her, a nervous wreck of a photographer kicked a fuse box, got a shock, fell ten feet and lay on the floor unconscious.

Someone ran to the studio medical office, and in a few moments the doctor arrived, kit in hand. He overlooked the injured man, darted to the bed, and doused the star's nostrils with ammonia. She jumped out of bed and ran around screaming. Someone ordered work ended in order to save a score of mild neurotics from becoming straitjacket cases. Goldwyn's unconquerable spirit failed him, and he never tried to make that particular scene again.

Sam does the best he can to make a picture right. After it is made, he usually accepts the verdict of the box office. Even two adverse verdicts did not convince him that he was wrong about Sten. He went on to make a third failure with her.

Goldwyn's expensive campaign to make the American public like Anna Sten might not have occurred except for his success ten years earlier with Vilma Banky. He discovered Miss Banky when he saw her picture in a photograph shop at Budapest. This was a feat, because, when the photograph was sent to Hollywood, the Goldwyn executives could see no possibilities in her. She arrived in Hollywood herself a few days after her photograph.

Miss Banky was still bewildered on her arrival in Hollywood. "I thought I was being tricked," she told an interpreter. "I didn't believe the man was Goldwyn until he gave me two thousand dollars." Sam had signed a contract in Budapest giving her $250 a week for the first year, with increases up to $750 a week for the fifth year.

After her enormous success in *The Dark Angel*, he voluntarily tore up the old contract and drew up a new one at $2000 a week, rising to $5000 a week on the fourth year. When Miss Banky married Rod La Roque, Sam took charge of the wedding and made it one of the most dignified and elegant in Hollywood history, up to the time when guests began to steal the floral decorations and the roast turkeys.

Sam's experience with Miss Banky was unfortunate in the end. Her accent was too broad for the talkies and she would not undergo the toil necessary to master English. Sam paid her about a quarter of a million dollars while she idled out the contract. By contrast Miss Banky reminds Sam of Geraldine Farrar, whom he regards as the woman of the ages; when Farrar found herself losing popularity and becoming a burden to her company, she tore up a contract which obligated Goldwyn to pay her $250,000.

Sam is a great detail man. Nothing is unimportant to him. He is a marvel on fine points of costuming. His rehabilitation of Montgomery, by changing his collar, is the sort of thing he does regularly on the Goldwyn lot. He has both art and box office in mind, but he would not permit a cheap or tin-horn effect in a Goldwyn picture, even if it could be mathematically demonstrated that the public would go wild about it. He will spend tens of thousands of dollars on obscure details that could not possibly cause the picture to sell one more ticket. In making one of his first talking pictures, Sam spent $20,-000 because of an unjust prejudice against a monosyllable. In a scene that was written by Sidney Howard, a waiter breaks the silence of a London club by dropping a spoon on the carpet; a startled clubman exclaims, "What is the meaning of this infernal din?"

Sam was pleased with the scene when he saw it in the projection room, but knitted his brows afterward and said: "There was a word that sounded to me like 'din.'" This was corroborated.

"What is that word 'din?'" asked Sam.

"It means 'noise.'"

"Then why didn't the writer say 'noise?'" demanded Sam. After thinking it over for a while, he ordered the entire scene remade. The settings had already been removed. Contracts with some of the actors had expired.

"It makes no difference," said Sam. "We have to reshoot it. The word is archaic."

Actors were rehired. The scene was set again. In the meantime, Sam had been telling everyone about the archaic word. Some great authority—said to be William Randolph Hearst—told him that "din" was not archaic, but was every bit as good as "noise." Sam then gave orders not to reshoot it.

Part of Sam's greatness is in a twilight state that he gets into while making a picture. During this period he is highly suggestible. He is likely to accept a fantastic suggestion, develop it still more fantastically, waste a small fortune on it and then suddenly come to his senses, exclaiming, "They're ruining me! Why do they do such things to me?" During this twilight state, a kind word will send Sam up into the clouds; a slur will chill his heart. He has always been that way. Arthur Hopkins quit Goldwyn eighteen years ago, saying, "I can't always be shooting up in the elevator or shooting down in it with Sam." During the suggestible state; Sam adopts suggestions so quickly that he seems to have originated them. An executive of Sam's was once asked what kind of man Goldwyn was. He replied, "Goldwyn is the kind of man who, if he understands what you tell him, thinks he thought of it himself." While he is in the fog, however, Sam is always ransacking other men's minds for "the Goldwyn touch." Patiently, diligently, he reaches into and searches $3000-a-week brains and $5000-a-week brains in the hope of finding something worthy of Goldwyn. He is a Flaubert—with the exception that the French genius tirelessly explored his own intellect for the perfect effect, while Goldwyn tirelessly explores the intellects that he has under contract. The results over a long period have justified Sam's methods. The percentage of ham in Goldwyn pictures is less than in those of any other producer. Not all of his pictures are masterpieces, but he commits few crimes against his own standards.

Sam is a spellbinder by telephone. If television arrives in time to let him transmit his hypnotic eye and his library of facial expressions, he will be greater than ever. As it is, even with the telephone in a rudimentary state, Sam can project a good deal of his personality over it. Writers have been shanghaied from New York to Hollywood by a few minutes of conversation with Goldwyn. They say "No" at first. Sam talks. Finally, they go as if extradited. Sometimes they struggle against their fate, but Sam rarely fails to get them in the long run.

Even with his business rivals and business enemies, Sam is a siren over the telephone. Executives in other companies wake up in a daze after a telephone conversation with Sam and dimly remember, to their dismay, that they have promised to lend him stars, directors or technical men. Sam once telephoned to David Selznick and asked to borrow George Cukor, one of the greatest of the directors. "Absolutely not," said Selznick, but he finally broke down and consented. Cukor, however, refused to work for Goldwyn. Then Sam telephoned to Selznick again; he wanted the reluctant Selznick to persuade the reluctant Cukor to direct a picture for Goldwyn. Cukor was firm. Sam finally had to confess defeat, and it was on this occasion that he said, "That's the way with these directors; they're always biting the hand that lays the golden egg."

Another one of Sam's infrequent repulses over the telephone occurred in a conversation with Louis B. Mayer, head of the Metro-Goldwyn-Mayer studio. Sam wanted to borrow two of M-G-M's big stars, but he did not open the conversation by saying so. He opened it by saying that he had been grieving because he had not seen Mayer for a long time, and that he was getting worried for fear that Louis was overworking and injuring his health. Mayer admitted that he was overworking and not feeling any too well. Sam cross-examined him as to the symptoms and then gave him a fatherly scolding, illustrated with homely maxims: Life is short. We live but once. Great men are rare; they owe a duty to the world to look after their health. There is a limit to human endurance. Nobody can drive himself at a terrific pace forever. Sam prescribed home remedies, rest, a change of doctors. He spent nearly fifteen minutes on the lecture on hygiene before he started a transition to the subject of borrowing two stars. Sam brought it in like an afterthought, a little notion that had suddenly struck him.

Mayer roared with indignation. A battle of epithets

followed. Sam had hardly finished dishing out health hints when he began to call down all sorts of afflictions and disasters on Mayer.

Edgar Selwyn, one of Sam's oldest friends, is a producer at the M-G-M studio. Their telephone conversation has a standard opening, as follows:

"Edgar, where have you been keeping yourself? Why don't I ever see you? How've you ——"

"What do you want, Sam?"

Sam protests a little, and then makes his request.

Sam loses his power when he has to write. He can't make words coo and purr and explode on paper. The glittering eye, the gestures, the ecstasy and despair, the magical sense of timing, cannot be translated into black and white. The Ancient Mariner had the Goldwyn approach; he would have lost his power if he had to send the Wedding Guest a memorandum.

When Sam works on an important letter or statement, he is likely to call in everyone on the lot to ghost for him, but no genius can get Sam's furious feelings on paper. Some of his publicity and advertising campaigns have been considered masterpieces, but Sam is rarely satisfied. He did praise one Goldwyn statement. Sam imported a famous advertising writer from New York who spent several days writing an eloquent proclamation of a new Goldwyn policy. Sam read it to his executives and said, "There. That sounds like me." He was pleased once with an advertisement of his picture, *We Live Again*, which read: "The directorial genius of Mamoulian, the beauty of Sten and the producing genius of Goldwyn have been combined to make the world's greatest entertainment."

"That," said Sam, "is the kind of ad I like. Facts. No exaggeration."

There is one instance on record of Sam's failing orally, and attempting to make his point by written words. He had just finished *Arrowsmith* and was trying to tell Helen Hayes how great it was. When his words and gestures failed to impress her, he said, "Come to my office. I want you to read a letter I wrote about it."

Sam had a long illness last year, but has regained his former vigorous health. During his sickness he planned to take life easier in the future; during his convalescence he outlined for himself the largest year's program that he had ever undertaken. He resolved also that he would be milder and gentler; that resolution stuck until he began to feel great.

Last year was Sam's twenty-third in the movie business; his press department at that time spotted him two years and celebrated the completion of his quarter century in the business. Next year is Sam's real silver jubilee. It is something for everybody to get patriotic about. The U. S. A. leads the world by a wider margin in pictures than anything else, and one of the chief reasons is the Great Goldwyn.

ASPECTS OF FILM

An Arno Press Collection

Adler, Mortimer J. **Art and Prudence.** 1937
Conant, Michael. **Anti-Trust in the Motion Picture Industry.** 1960
Croy, Homer. **How Motion Pictures Are Made.** 1918
Drinkwater, John. **The Life and Adventures of Carl Laemmle.** 1931
Hacker, Leonard. **Cinematic Design.** 1931
Hepworth, T[homas] C[raddock]. **The Book of the Lantern.** 1899
Johnston, Alva. **The Great Goldwyn.** 1937
Klingender, F.D. and Stuart Legg. **Money Behind the Screen.** 1937
Limbacher, James L. **Four Aspects of the Film.** 1969
Manvell, Roger, ed. **The Cinema 1950.** 1950
Manvell, Roger, ed. **The Cinema 1951.** 1951
Manvell, Roger, ed. **The Cinema 1952.** 1952
Marchant, James, ed. **The Cinema in Education.** 1925
Mayer, J.P. **British Cinemas and Their Audiences.** 1948
Sabaneev, Leonid. **Music for the Films.** 1935
Seabury, William Marston. **Motion Picture Problems.** 1929
Seldes, Gilbert. **The Movies Come from America.** 1937
U.S. House of Representatives, Committee on Education. **Motion Picture Commission: Hearings.** 1914
U.S. House of Representatives, Committee on Education. **Federal Motion Picture Commission: Hearings.** 1916
U.S. Senate, Temporary National Economic Committee. **Investigation of Concentration of Economic Power.** 1941
Weinberg, Herman G. **Josef von Sternberg.** 1967